Praise for *Amplify*

Amplify is essential reading for anyone serious about performance leadership. It brings rare clarity to the realities of leading in high-stakes environments — where the pressure is constant, but so is the potential.

Across three decades in sport, governance and global leadership, I've been part of transformative system shifts — from athlete well-being and integrity reform, to advancing women in leadership, designing national programmes and leading major venue and stadium developments. At the heart of it all has been a commitment to building systems that enable people and teams to thrive, perform and succeed on the world stage. I recognise the depth in this book because I've lived the realities it speaks to.

Richard has created a powerful resource — one that distils the complexity of sustained high-performance leadership into something deeply usable, clear and relevant. *Amplify* combines lived experience, thoughtful insight and a strong structural backbone that helps leaders not only sharpen their thinking, but strengthen how they lead.

I'll be coming back to it often — *Amplify* sharpens your edge and keeps you leading where it matters most. It's a leadership essential!

— **Kereyn Smith CNZM**
Chair, The Eden Park Trust Board; Former CEO and Secretary General, New Zealand Olympic Committee; Vice President, Commonwealth Sport; Global Advocate for Women in Sport and Leadership

If you're serious about leading and delivering higher performance, then *Amplify* is essential reading.

Richard has delivered again. This book is packed with practical insights that unpack the real keys to performance leadership. He skillfully balances lived experience with evidence-based thinking — making the complex simple and the abstract actionable.

Amplify is a timely reminder that leadership is defined by action, not by title. In particular, action aligned to purpose. Purpose is fixed, but how we realise it must remain fluid. Richard brings this to life with precision — the more we add, the more we clutter. The less we simplify, the less we execute.

Great leaders empower, not control, because control is often just a poor reaction to pressure. As *Amplify* shows, sustained performance depends on simplicity, alignment and well-being.

This is a book I'll return to often. I hope you get as much value from it as I did.

— Don Tricker ONZM
World champion coach; former High Performance Manager at New Zealand Rugby; Director of Player Health and Performance, San Diego Padres

Amplify is an outstanding read. It's a complete guide to performance leadership. Richard Young has taken decades of elite sport experience and translated it into leadership insights that are deeply practical and powerfully relevant. The analogies are sharp, the structure is clean and the principles are built to last.

This book holds up both a mirror and a map. It helps you see where you are as a leader and where you could go if you choose to lead with clarity, consistency and intent. From clarity traps to performance well-being, *Amplify* is full of ideas that prompt reflection and drive action.

What sets *Amplify* apart is how it connects the dots between your role as a leader, the environment you shape and the culture you sustain. Richard addresses the central challenge of modern leadership, which is how to build performance that endures. Beyond results — it's about creating the systems, the people and the conditions that make those results inevitable.

This is a book about legacy and setting a foundation for success that lasts. Having spent a lifetime in elite sport, I can say without hesitation that this is the clearest and most compelling synthesis of what drives sustained performance I've read. Richard has achieved what few others manage: he makes the complex feel simple and the simple feel profound.

— **Alex Baumann OC**
Double Olympic gold medallist and former
double world record holder; former CEO of high
performance sport in Canada, New Zealand and
Australia; former CEO of Swimming Australia

Amplify is a standout read and a must-have for any leader's bookshelf. It is engaging, insightful and packed with practical nuggets that will resonate with anyone committed to leadership and personal growth. It builds brilliantly on Richard's first book, *Simplify*. Once again, he's delivered a thoughtful and powerful contribution to the leadership space.

Having worked with Richard during my time at Cycling New Zealand, I saw firsthand his ability to weave together insights from great leadership thinkers and mentors, while adding his own depth and clarity. I've read many related leadership books, including *The Chimp Paradox* by Steve Peters, *Start with Why* by Simon Sinek, *Dare to Lead* by Brené Brown and *Legacy* by James Kerr. *Amplify* brings many of the best ideas together in one place and adds fresh, original wisdom.

For me, the standout concepts in *Amplify* are the Three Lights of Leadership paradigm and the Simplicity, Alignment and Well-being system. These are innovative and practical, making this book an essential addition to any leader's library.

— Jacques Landry
Director, UCI World Cycling Centre (Centre Mondial du Cyclisme – CMC), Lausanne, Switzerland

After more than 30 years immersed in high performance — as an Olympian, advocate and leader — I've seen what separates good leadership from great. It's not just what you do; it's how and why you do it. That's exactly what *Amplify* captures.

Richard has distilled decades of lived experience and deep observation into something rare: a guide that speaks to leaders at every level. Whether you're stepping into a new role or have been in the arena for decades, this book meets you where you are.

What I value most is how *Amplify* prompts reflection without judgement. It's a practical companion for leaders who want to grow with intention — to check in on their blind spots and also acknowledge their wisdom and progress.

I'll be using *Amplify* regularly — not as a manual, but as a mirror. One that reminds us all how to lead with clarity, energy and purpose. This is a vital read for anyone serious about sustained high performance.

— Barbara Kendall CNZM, MBE, OLY
Five-time Olympian, three-time Olympic medallist;
former IOC member and global advocate
for athlete and women's leadership

Amplify is leadership clarity at its best.

Richard shows how it's done. He knows how to get to the heart of challenging leadership issues in simple, concise language and clear structure. He uses profound metaphors and analogies to help you understand and design performance-enhancing systems. Building on the foundation of his first book, *Simplify*, Richard adds depth to mastery and antifragility into his leadership approach. It is concise and practical at the same time.

From firsthand experience, I know that this approach transfers fast and delivers success. If you want leadership that lasts, start here.

— Olav Spahl
High Performance Director, Belgian Olympic Committee;
Chef de Mission for Team Belgium (Tokyo 2020, Beijing 2022,
Paris 2024, Milano Cortina 2026); former Head of Olympic
Training Centres, German Olympic Sports Confederation

If you care about leadership that holds up under pressure, read this book.

In *Amplify*, Richard Young has done something rare — he's captured the essence of performance leadership in a way that is both deeply grounded in lived experience and immediately usable under real-world pressure. Having worked with elite performers across Formula 1, Olympic sport, military training and corporate leadership, I've seen that most ideas crumble under pressure when theory meets reality. Richard's don't, because they were forged in it.

One of the book's greatest strengths is its clarity and simplicity. In an age overloaded with content and complexity, *Amplify* cuts straight to what matters. You won't find abstract leadership jargon here. It's a playbook of practical insights backed by decades inside some of the most demanding environments.

Whether you're leading a boardroom, an organisation or a national programme, *Amplify* offers something invaluable: a mirror to clarify how you lead — and a map to align, sharpen and fine-tune your impact. This isn't about adding noise. It's about raising your signal.

Keep this book close. It's a leadership edge.

— **Dr Kerry Spackman**
Cognitive neuroscientist and author of
***The Winner's Bible*; advisor to Formula 1 champions,**
Olympic teams and global executives

Amplify nails the reality of high performance — dynamic, unpredictable and often chaotic. Richard captures what it really takes to lead in that space: clarity under pressure, constant decision-making and a leader-leader mindset.

This isn't about chasing outcomes — it's about the relentless application of behaviours that drive performance, especially when the path isn't clear. From navigating incomplete data to reframing and going again, this book shows how high performers stay in motion and stay effective.

Amplify is a must-read for anyone leading in high-pressure environments — whether you're just starting out or already deep in it.

Having led performance strategy across some of the UK's most successful teams and organisations, I recognise the power of these insights. *Amplify* offers a fresh, honest perspective on the real world of high performance — in sport and far beyond.

— Dr Scott Drawer
Performance Director at INEOS Grenadiers; former Head of Team Sky Performance Hub; former Head of Research & Innovation at UK Sport; former Head of Performance Pathways at England Rugby

What a read! Loved it. A rollicking, energising journey that speaks to the heart of real leadership.

You can feel Richard's passion and enthusiasm for high performance. He is hungry to learn and to keep learning. Fortunately for the rest of us, he also has that delicious drive to generously share.

Richard knows where the leverage lies – in the personal practical knowledge (PPK) of those who live high performance. Interviewing, listening, questioning and observing are at the core of his work. Seldom do we get access to such gold.

Leading is about aligning to a vision, crystal clarity about the underpinning mental models and then designing and implementing the systems and structures needed to live out those mental models to bring the vision to reality. Richard takes us through these phases in detail through his high performance examples.

Everyone leads. Understanding this and balancing our autonomy with the autonomy of those around us is complex. Living the complexity of this responsibility is one of the joys of high performance. This book wraps us in example after example of what this looks like and feels like.

Any reader is going to be challenged to stop regularly, reflect on their own PPK and explore deeply. You won't escape unaffected. This is the power of *Amplify*.

— Dr John Edwards
Leadership strategist and systems thinker; co-founder of Edwards & Associates; international advisor on leadership and organisational development; co-author of *Schools That Deliver*

Amplify is the book I wish every coach, athlete and leader had in their hands — not just because it's insightful, but because it's usable. It shows you what high performance really looks like behind the curtain and how to lead it from the inside out.

Even from our early days on the road together, it was clear that Richard was intensely observant and intrepidly curious about high performance. And he's absolutely hilarious to boot! That mindset has since evolved into a deep, nuanced understanding of what sets high performers apart. In *Amplify*, Richard distils the intricacies of high performance into a clear, practical guide. It's a book you'll return to — whether you're a student eager to apply these lessons to your own journey, or a seasoned pro in need of a reminder of what it took to get there. If performance matters to you, this book should be on your desk.

— Curt Harnett
Three-time Olympic medallist, former world record holder; Olympic Chef de Mission, Member of the Order of Canada, Managing Director at World Bicycle Relief

Amplify delivers a clear, practical and repeatable framework for leadership and lasting achievement. Richard Young's approach is grounded in principles and enriched by decades of experience in high performance, making this a powerful guide to sustained success — whether in sport, business or life. As someone who has coached both men's and women's teams at Olympic, professional and NCAA collegiate levels, I recognise the depth and clarity this book brings to real-world leadership. I highly recommend it.

— Hugh McCutcheon MNZM
Secretary General, International Volleyball Federation (FIVB); Olympic gold and silver medal–winning coach; International Volleyball Hall of Fame inductee; author of *Championship Behaviors*

If you're serious about leading people — not just managing them — *Amplify* gives you a system to build clarity, momentum and impact in any environment.

We often forget the role sport plays in teaching the skills that matter most in leadership — decision-making under pressure, communication that cuts through and the discipline to keep showing up. In *Amplify*, Richard Young highlights the proven strategies from elite sport that can help build and sustain a performance mindset in teams, organisations and leadership.

This book will resonate particularly with those transitioning into leadership roles — whether you've come from sport or not. That's because it's practical, grounded and full of moments that prompt real reflection.

Amplify is the kind of book that doesn't just sit on a shelf — it shapes how you show up as a leader.

— Marco di Buono
President, Canadian Tire Jumpstart Charities

Amplify is one of the most grounded and insightful books I've read on what real leadership looks like under pressure. It captures the truth about performance leadership — that it's not about charisma or control, but clarity, consistency and conviction.

Over the years, I've worked with and learned from some of the best leaders in Olympic sport. The ones who truly elevated those around them were never the loudest in the room — they were the ones who created environments where people felt seen, trusted and expected to rise.

Richard Young understands this deeply. In *Amplify*, he offers a rare blend of high-performance insight and human connection. This book helps you see what separates the leaders who create short-term results from those who build long-term legacy.

If you lead — or aspire to — and care about doing it well, *Amplify* belongs on your shelf. Or, better yet, in your hands.

— Duff Gibson
Winter Olympic gold medallist; author of *The Tao of Sport*

Amplify is an incredibly powerful and thought-provoking book. Having had the privilege of working with Richard as a mentor, I was genuinely excited to dive into this.

The title perfectly captures the essence and impact of the content. This is a must-read for anyone striving to build and sustain high-performing environments. Richard has managed to distil the critical elements of performance into a clear, accessible framework that equips coaches and leaders with the tools they need to thrive.

His extensive experience across Olympic programs shines through, providing rich, real-world examples that highlight the nuances of roles, environments and what it truly takes to deliver under pressure.

Amplify is more than a book — it's a performance compass. For professionals serious about leading with clarity, conviction and purpose, this is essential reading.

— Cory Sweeney
Head Coach, Black Ferns Sevens; double Olympic medallist, Commonwealth Games gold medallist, World Series champion

AMPLIFY

AMPLIFY

THE KEYS TO PERFORMANCE LEADERSHIP
LESSONS FROM HIGH PERFORMANCE SPORT

RICHARD YOUNG PHD

Published by Richard Young

First published in 2025 in Dunedin, New Zealand

Copyright © Richard Young

https://simplify2perform.com

https://richardnyoung.com

All rights reserved. No part of this book may be reproduced, stored in a retrieval system or transmitted in any form or by any means, electronic, mechanical, photocopying, recording or otherwise, without the prior written permission of the publisher, except as provided by New Zealand copyright law.

Disclaimer

The material in this publication is of the nature of general comment only and does not represent professional advice. It is not intended to provide specific guidance for particular circumstances, and it should not be relied on as the basis for any decision to take action or not to take action on any matter which it covers. Readers should obtain professional advice where appropriate, before making any such decision. To the maximum extent permitted by law, the author and publisher disclaim all responsibility and liability to any person, arising directly or indirectly from any person taking or not taking action based on the information in this publication.

All inquiries should be made to the author.

Edited by Jenny Magee

Designed and typeset in Australia by BookPOD

Printed in New Zealand by PHPrint

ISBN: 978-1-0670692-0-9 (paperback)
ISBN: 978-1-0670692-1-6 (e-book)

For Ollie, Gracie, Emily-Rose and Leo — my greatest examples of what it means to lead with heart, live with grace and lift others as you go.

ACKNOWLEDGEMENTS

This book was forged in a different kind of fire.

Since writing *Simplify*, life has changed in ways I never expected. My wife, Donna, passed away suddenly from illness. We found ourselves in a perfect storm — me and our four kids — navigating the heartbreak of loss while isolated through the stillness of COVID. It was a time when the world went quiet and our grief was deafening.

In that space, we became an even closer team — not by design, but by necessity. A tightly bound crew, learning together, breaking down, building up and moving forward. This book carries all of that. It carries her. Donna was a beautiful soul and a wonderful award winning writer. She was exceptional at exploring meaning to find the story beneath the story. This is my offering to that belief, and to her.

To those who showed up in this chapter of life — thank you. Paul Caldwell, Tom Heath (you never walk alone), Pete Gallagher, Caroline Young, Elaine Rutherford, Flossy Hinton and the Rutherford, Webb, Southey and Renzetti families — your presence, conversations and encouragement lifted us at just the right time.

To the world-class minds who shifted my understanding of leadership and performance: Richie Poulton, Dean Spitzer,

Don Tricker, Hubert and Stuart Dreyfus, Patricia Benner, Kerry Spackman, Alex Baumann, Kereyn Smith, Katie Sadleir, Matt Church, Robert Fritz, John Edwards, Pete Pfitzinger, Chris Bullen, Marty Toomey, Hugh McCutcheon — your influence runs deep in these pages.

To the wider high-performance community — the coaches, athletes, support staff and leaders who invited me into your world — thank you. The work you do and the way you think continue to challenge and refine mine.

To Jenny Magee, my brilliant editor, who helped shape this book with expert precision and care.

To my kids. Thank you for holding each other and for holding me. Your kindness, care and unwavering love have been my greatest teachers. The strength and courage you've carried through loss is the quiet power behind every page of this book. You are my best role models in what personal leadership truly means.

And to you, the reader. Whether you're leading teams, nurturing talent, navigating change or simply trying to find your next step, I hope something in these pages helps you do it with greater clarity, deeper courage and a stronger sense of meaning.

This book is about performance — but at its heart, it's about people. It's about you.

FOREWORD

Leadership today is more demanding, more exposed and arguably more consequential than it's ever been. In a time when many seek clarity, confidence and direction, *Amplify* offers something rare — not just a set of ideas, but a complete reset. It prompts leaders at every level to reflect deeply, act wisely and lead in ways that last. This book arrived at just the right time, and I believe it will leave a lasting impact.

I've spent over three decades working in and around high-performance environments — as an athlete, in senior leadership roles and now as CEO of Commonwealth Sport. Along the way I've been fortunate to work with many remarkable leaders and contribute to meaningful change across sport and governance. But what I've learned, more than anything, is that lasting leadership isn't about visibility or volume — it's about stewardship. That's why *Amplify* struck such a deep chord.

One idea Richard captures so clearly is that **stewardship is legacy.** It's a call to act. Whether we're leading a programme, a team, an organisation or a global event, the responsibility is the same: leave it better than you found it. Build systems where others can thrive. Create cultures where the right things are done the right way at the right time. That's what great leaders do. They don't chase the moment, they shape what comes next.

Richard Young has long been one of the clearest voices in the performance and leadership space. I first worked alongside him in New Zealand during our time with High Performance Sport NZ and the Academy of Sport. Even then it was clear that Richard saw what others missed. He brought evidence, reflection and simplicity to complexity. *Amplify* brings all of that thinking together in a way that is accessible, tested and ready to be applied.

I see the themes in this book play out every day. Over the past decade, I've taken on some of the biggest challenges of my career, helping lead the global transformation of women's rugby at World Rugby and, more recently, navigating the shifting landscape of the Commonwealth Games as CEO of the Federation. From urgent crises like the sudden withdrawal of the Victoria Games to the high-pressure, fast-paced challenge of reimagining a new Games model, success has depended on one constant: distributed leadership showing up — in the boardroom, on the ground and across the field of play.

That's exactly what *Amplify* speaks to. It doesn't place leadership in one person's hands. It spreads it. It challenges the outdated idea that performance comes from the top and shows what happens when leadership is shared, lived and reinforced in daily behaviours. Richard explains this with clarity and with real humility. He recognises that leadership is not about knowing all the answers. It's about noticing what matters, deciding with purpose and helping others do the same.

Reading this book was like returning to the conversations that matter most — the kind that stay with you long after the meeting ends. The kind that make you stop, take a breath and think differently.

The reflections throughout *Amplify* are powerful on their own. But the way they are paired with real questions, tested practices and repeatable habits make this more than a book — it's a toolkit. One you'll return to, share and grow with.

Along the way in my career, I've been honoured to receive recognition — from a CNZM for my contribution to women in sport and governance, to the KEA World Class New Zealander Award and the Lincoln University International Medal. While those awards are humbling, they also remind me of the environments, challenges and people that shaped them. *Amplify* captures the essence of that journey — the unseen work, the shared responsibility and the systems we build to outlast us.

Whether you lead in sport, business, education or community, I can't recommend this book enough. It will challenge you, equip you and remind you why you lead in the first place. If you're looking to lead with more clarity, more meaning and more lasting impact, then start here.

Katie Sadleir CNZM
Chief Executive Officer,
Commonwealth Sport; Olympian;
Commonwealth Games medallist;
World Class New Zealander;
champion of women in sport and leadership

CONTENTS

A Roadmap for Performance Leadership ... 1

Part One: The World of High Performance — 9

- Chapter 1 Understanding High Performance ... 11
- Chapter 2 The Challenge ... 15
- Chapter 3 The Performance System ... 21
- Chapter 4 The Performer ... 27
- Chapter 5 The Podium ... 33
- Chapter 6 Sustaining High Performance ... 39

Part Two: The Foundations of High Performance — 45

- Chapter 7 Your Game of Experience, Essence, Excellence and Empowerment ... 47
- Chapter 8 Awareness and Its Black Arrow ... 53
- Chapter 9 The Three Lights of Leadership ... 61
- Chapter 10 The Engine of Excellence ... 69
- Chapter 11 Fit-ness for Empowerment ... 73
- Chapter 12 Craft Mastery ... 77
- Chapter 13 Mana ... 83
- Chapter 14 The Power of 10% ... 87

Part Three: Unlocking High Performance — 95

    Chapter 15 Leaders, Learners, Performers and Contributors — 97

    Chapter 16 Leaders — 101

    Chapter 17 Learners — 107

    Chapter 18 Performers — 115

    Chapter 19 Contributors — 121

Part Four: Sustaining High Performance — 131

    Chapter 20 Three Pillars of Sustained Success — 133

    Chapter 21 Well-being Brings Energy — 137

    Chapter 22 Simplicity Brings Clarity — 147

    Chapter 23 Alignment Brings Cohesion — 159

    Chapter 24 The Sustained Performance Game — 169

Part Five: Tools and Traps — 179

    Chapter 25 Alignment Traps — 181

    Chapter 26 Clarity Traps — 185

    Chapter 27 Energy Traps — 189

    Chapter 28 A Call to Performance Leadership — 195

Support From Here — 200

Meet Richard Young — 202

Further Reading — 204

References — 206

A ROADMAP FOR PERFORMANCE LEADERSHIP

Performance leadership transcends the realms of sports and business, distinguishing high-achieving teams and systems from the rest.

With decades of experience participating, observing and supporting Olympic athletes, leaders and experts, I know that high-performance sport has much to teach business and leaders in any field. The parallels of excellence are there — if you know where to look.

My last book, *Simplify*, focused on the systems that underpin high performance. It echoed the belief of author James Clear that 'You do not rise to the level of your goals; you fall to the level of your systems'.[1]

Systems are, indeed, crucial. But it is performance *leadership* — intentional, personal decision-making in every moment — that unlocks exceptional team performance. It's time to take that next step.

That's what this book, *Amplify*, is about. Identifying and overcoming what holds teams and organisations back from sustained high performance. You may have world-class systems, but the success you seek will remain elusive unless you implement the key drivers that deliver performance leadership.

Amplify is a playbook for guiding you and your team to unparalleled success. Performance leadership is based on medallist and non-medallist research over 11 Olympic cycles and tested across more than 50 sports in seven countries. In these pages, you'll learn about strategic simplicity, anti-fragility, role alignment, performance well-being and more, all converging to optimise your performance system and leadership.

Whether on the field, in the office or at home, these insights will shape you, your team and your system into a consistent competitive advantage.

Where this book will take you

The chapters are arranged in five parts that build on each other.

Part One: The World of High Performance introduces the core concepts of what high performance truly means and how leadership shapes systems.

Part Two: The Foundations of High Performance dives into the practical steps, building habits and enabling empowerment.

Part Three: Unlocking High Performance explores the mindset shifts and roles of leader, learner, contributor and performer that sustain adaptability and resilience.

Part Four: Sustaining High Performance focuses on performance well-being, simplicity, alignment and building anti-fragile systems and environments that endure.

Part Five: Tools, Traps and Transformation examines common pitfalls and challenges.

Parts One to Four conclude with a **Summary Guide** that includes the key ideas, blind spots and amplifying questions. Leadership requires action, so embrace these exercises. The more you reflect and apply your knowledge, the deeper the transformation.

Loss and learning

The chapters ahead will walk you through the patterns, principles and systems that drive high performance. Before we dive in, I want to share how this all began — not in theory, but in practice. Behind every insight in this book is lived experience: hard-won lessons from the track, the boardroom and beyond.

The story that follows isn't just where it all started. It's where everything changed. It's the turning point — the moment when everything I thought I knew about performance fell apart and what I discovered in the aftermath.

The push

I think in four-year cycles. I have since I was five — wide-eyed and captivated, watching the Olympics on TV. There was something about the scale of it all: the precision, the pressure, the convergence of the world's best on a single stage, at a single time. Even then, I wasn't just watching sport — I was studying it.

That sparked something in me — a lifelong fascination with high performance and what it takes to thrive when it counts most.

AMPLIFY

I fell in love with cycling and progressed to the national team for Canada. The dream of the Olympics was lit.

Soon every breath, every decision, every dream was fixed on one goal: making the Canadian Olympic cycling team.

In 1982 I left Toronto for Montreal, chasing a shot at something bigger at the country's only indoor velodrome. I enrolled at McGill, but, in truth, school came second. My life was training — three sessions a day, every day, because more felt better. Every day was a push toward Los Angeles.

I was already chasing marginal gains before that phrase was even trendy — drilling holes into expensive components to shave grams off the bike, filling tyres with helium, tweaking anything that might move the needle. If I read about a new technology, I tried it — or built it. Everything seemed like a good idea.

When the Soviet boycott reshaped the 1984 Olympics, Canada could send a bigger team and decided to send a B team. I wasn't just hopeful — I was ready. I'd earned my spot as the second sprinter behind Curt Harnett, already one of Canada's rising stars.

Then came the airport.

The coaches called us together. Their faces were blank, unreadable. A pause — too long. Then: *'Only the A team is going. No B team. No reserves'.*

Just like that, the door slammed shut.

I stood there holding my plane ticket. Frozen. Every pre-dawn ride, every compromise, every sacrifice was gone. I'd given everything to a system that, in a heartbeat, gave nothing back.

Two days later, a second blow: a letter from McGill. I'd failed out. No third year. No degree. No Olympics. No fallback. No plan B.

Rock bottom was in my parents' basement. I sat there in the dark, staring at a knife. Cold. Heavy. Final.

Failure. Shame. Emptiness. The system had collapsed. But I hadn't yet realised the system inside me had too. No structure. No resilience. Just silence.

Then I saw a photo taped to the wall — a family camping trip with all of us around the fire, roasting marshmallows. No medals. Just joy. That version of me didn't need a result to feel whole. In that memory I sensed an opening.

I lifted my eyes and threw the knife across the room.

It wasn't clarity. It wasn't resolution. But it was a response. And it was enough to lift me. Quietly and unexpectedly, it gave me something to stand on and move forward from.

Looking back, it's easy to say the system failed me. Maybe it did. But it also revealed something I couldn't have seen otherwise: when the external structures fall apart, the internal ones matter even more.

Performance leadership isn't tested when things are working. It's tested when they are not.

The pull

I had built my life around the single belief that if you worked hard enough, success was inevitable. But now I wasn't so sure.

I made a deal with McGill. I told them the Olympic dream hadn't worked out and committed to pulling my average back up. If I couldn't, I'd leave. With that commitment, I threw myself into my physiology studies with the same intensity I had once reserved for the track.

I returned to cycling — but this time I wasn't just chasing performance. I was studying it.

One question consumed me. *Why do some athletes and teams keep winning while others fade away?*

At the 1988 Olympics, I qualified as a reserve behind Curt Harnett, who was already an Olympic medallist from LA. My job was to be ready if needed, to push and support him in training, and to learn.

> **Performance systems create stability. Performance leadership creates results.**

I attacked the question the way I once attacked the track. I devoured books, rewound race footage and interviews frame by frame, and cornered champions and their coaches anywhere they would talk. In dining halls and on buses, I asked, *'What made the difference for you?'* Their answers varied, but patterns emerged that were powerful and undeniable.

It became clear that sustained success isn't about talent alone. It comes from something deeper — structure, clarity, connection and personal leadership. All by design.

Performance systems create stability. Performance leadership creates results.

While others measured wins, I was mapping what made them repeatable. That pull became a pursuit — not just to understand performance, but to decode it. To cut through the noise, find the patterns that matter, and deliver results — faster, repeatably and sustainably.

The code

It became my professional work: collecting stories and data, distilling millions of words across decades to uncover the patterns that consistently lift performance at the highest level.

I interviewed every Olympic coach in British sport. I helped design innovation programmes for more than 40 sports in Great Britain and New Zealand. I rebuilt New Zealand's learning system across all Olympic sports. Along the way, I've worked with — and learned from — some of the best performance minds and leaders on the planet.

Now, I apply the same thinking internationally — from Olympic campaigns to boardrooms and leadership teams. The core principles are the same: people thrive when performance is led well.

I've had the privilege of sharing these patterns with world-class performers and leaders. Time and again, I hear the same thing: *'That's exactly how it works. I just wish I'd seen it sooner.'*

Now I'm sharing these patterns with you. This book begins with my story and carries the stories of many others — but at its heart, it's about yours. It's here to help you create, shape and accelerate your own path.

Welcome to *Amplify*.

PART ONE

THE WORLD OF HIGH PERFORMANCE

AMPLIFY

The following six chapters explore the baseline concepts that define *high performance*.

High performers have fewer blind spots, including the definitions of the key components that make up the starting point.

We'll examine what podium-level leadership entails, how to differentiate short-term gains from sustainable excellence and why systems, guided by personal accountability, drive results.

You'll meet key frameworks such as problem literacy, performance literacy and the importance of aligning purpose with daily habits.

CHAPTER 1

UNDERSTANDING HIGH PERFORMANCE

When people hear the term 'high performance', they often think of medals, titles and victories. But true high performance isn't defined by results; it's about the approach. The deliberate process that consistently produces excellence.

High performance is a daily decision. Results are simply the by-product of a well-executed system, and the personal leadership within it. High performance is a system of leadership committed to doing the right things, in the right way, at the right time.

> **High performance is a daily decision.**

Beyond medals

Imagine this: You've trained for years, pouring everything into a single moment. And then, by the slimmest of margins, you fall short. That's exactly what happened to one Olympic athlete I worked with. She missed a medal by fractions of a second. Sitting with her afterwards, I heard the devastation in her voice as she whispered, 'I've let everyone down.'

But she hadn't. Her performance was extraordinary, her personal best under immense pressure. What struck me was not her loss but the legacy of her effort. She had elevated her team and inspired others in ways that a medal could never define.

That moment taught me the enduring truth that high performance is more than a single achievement. It takes consistency, clarity and commitment to every step of the process. The renowned coach John Wooden said, 'Success is peace of mind, which is a direct result of self-satisfaction in knowing you made the effort to become the best you are capable of becoming.'

> **Success is peace of mind.**

The system behind success

High performance doesn't happen by chance. It's the result of systems designed to eliminate distractions, focus on essentials and create an environment where excellence thrives. Think of it like building a race car where every component must align perfectly for peak performance.

Simon Sinek puts it simply in *Start with Why*.[2]

'People don't buy what you do; they buy why you do it.' High performers know their 'why'. This clarity drives their habits, decisions and resilience. In sports, it might mean prioritising foundational skills over marginal gains. In business, that means cutting through unnecessary complexity to focus on what truly matters.

Build for the long term

High performance is a long game. Quick wins may feel satisfying, but they rarely lead to sustained success. One team I worked with constantly shifted their strategies, chasing every new trend. The result? Exhaustion and inconsistency. Compare this to the New Zealand All Blacks rugby team, who emphasise legacy and long-term development. Their ethos, 'Better people make better All Blacks', reflects a focus on culture and growth rather than immediate results.

In sports, business and life, sustainable systems prioritise long-term excellence over fleeting victories. They're built on a foundation of clarity, consistency and values.

What high performance means

High performance is not just what you achieve; it's how you achieve it. It's about building a process aligned with your values and purpose, one that ensures consistent growth and fulfilment. Think of high performance as a journey for life. It's a commitment to excellence in every action, decision and interaction.

Ask yourself:

- *What does high performance mean to you?*
- *Is it about a single moment of glory, or the legacy you build for you and others through consistent effort?*

Up next, we'll explore the challenge of not just achieving high performance but *maintaining* it. How do leaders cut through noise and distractions to preserve the energy and focus that drive success?

CHAPTER 2

THE CHALLENGE

Beyond the surface

There is high performance and then there is the challenge of maintaining and sustaining it. That is our call. Sustaining high performance is like climbing Everest; it's a sustained challenge that demands not just effort but strategy, alignment and clarity.

That doesn't mean grinding harder or repeating past successes. It's about identifying and solving the hidden complications and friction points that sabotage long-term results. While grit and practice may drive initial achievement, sustaining success requires a deeper understanding of what truly matters.

Leaders often fall victim to distractions, chasing short-term wins, mistaking activity for progress or succumbing to complacency. These aren't just obstacles; they're blind spots that sap energy and divert focus. Exceptional leaders rise above by cutting through the noise, zeroing in on the critical few, the vital 20% or even the defining 10%, that drive championship-level success. This chapter explores how to sharpen your focus, prioritise effectively and tackle the unseen challenges that disrupt sustained excellence.

Problem literacy is the true challenge

Performance leaders don't just solve problems — they know which ones matter. In sports, we have a set date, rules and insight into our competition. In business, the landscape is unclear, yet many chase high performance without defining the real problems — like assembling a thousand-piece puzzle without a picture.

> **Performance leaders solve problems that matter.**

Einstein said it best. 'If I had an hour to solve a problem, I'd spend 55 minutes thinking about the problem and five minutes thinking about solutions.' This is *problem literacy* — the ability to focus on the challenges that truly move the needle.

We don't have forever. Deadlines are real, competition is fierce and distractions are everywhere. Not every problem is worth solving. The best leaders identify and can easily describe the *big rocks* as the key issues that unlock progress.

Many struggle to answer the question, *'What are the basics?'* The answer is often, *'It depends'.* While context matters, success follows universal principles: identify the problems that matter most, focus here and remove distractions to act with precision. Those who master problem literacy move faster, waste less and get better results.

Preparation literacy builds an unshakeable foundation

Once the right problems are identified and clarified, preparation for action is the next frontier. Preparation literacy involves developing systems, routines and habits that make success inevitable. Like a solid house foundation, these elements provide resilience and stability under pressure.

Olympic champions credit their success not to last-minute heroics but to the unshakeable basics built over years of preparation. One gold medallist explained, 'Success comes naturally when your basics are rock-solid. If something goes wrong, I always know where to return'. Think of this like Hansel and Gretel's breadcrumb trail. Clear markers that guide you back to your foundations, enabling refinement without losing sight of what works.

> **'Success comes naturally when your basics are rock-solid.'**

The rhizome network is a powerful metaphor for high-performance preparation because it highlights the unseen, interconnected foundation that fuels explosive growth when the conditions are right. A rhizome is an underground root system that spreads laterally, often lying dormant or growing imperceptibly beneath the surface before suddenly producing visible shoots. That is what makes plants like bamboo, ginger and ferns so resilient. While they may appear static on the surface, below ground, they are expanding, strengthening and preparing for a moment of rapid emergence.

High-performance preparation mirrors this process. Unlike surface-level training that produces quick but unsustainable bursts of performance, systemic preparation embeds deep principles, habits and adaptive strategies long before they are needed. Champions and elite teams cultivate an ecosystem of excellence — routines, mindsets and environments that create an unshakable foundation.

When the moment comes, those who have built their preparation like a rhizome network, surge. Their growth is not accidental; it is the result of years of disciplined investment, adaptability and unseen work. True high-performance leaders don't just prepare for what is predictable — they build systems that allow them to thrive in uncertainty, just as the rhizome ensures a plant can regenerate even after adversity.

Performance literacy means thriving under pressure

Many people possess deep knowledge, but few can deliver excellence under pressure. The difference between a knowledge expert and a high-performance expert is the finish — the ability to execute with precision when the stakes are highest. Knowledge experts accumulate and refine information; high-performance experts transform knowledge into action, producing results in real time, under real pressure, when failure is not an option.

> **Performance leaders thrive in uncertainty.**

Performance literacy is more than just knowing — it's about adapting, responding and executing with clarity when everything is on the line. Those who master it have an unbreakable game, built through relentless exposure to high-stakes moments.

High-performance experts develop an unbreakable game, a mindset and skill set that ensures they deliver, no matter the conditions. Rather than crumbling, their expertise surfaces under pressure.

The best leaders and athletes understand this truth: You don't rise to the occasion; you fall to the level of your preparation.

That's what separates a knowledge expert from a performance expert — the ability to finish, to execute, to deliver when it counts.

You don't rise to the occasion; you fall to the level of your preparation.

Thriving in the challenge

Sustaining high performance is an ongoing process that balances problem literacy (knowing what matters), preparation literacy (doing what matters) and performance literacy (adapting when it matters most). The best have exceptional literacy in these three domains.

By recognising and focusing on the critical few — the defining 10% — performance leaders build systems that are resilient, adaptive and capable of sustained excellence. In the chapters ahead, we'll uncover actionable strategies to identify and master that 10%, build unshakeable preparation systems and cultivate the mindset needed to lead and thrive under pressure.

We've introduced the idea of focusing on the critical few. Next, we'll dive into the concept of the performance system, which determines whether you sustain or oscillate.

CHAPTER 3

THE PERFORMANCE SYSTEM

A performance system is the foundation of sustained high achievement. I'm not talking about tools like databases, CRMs or spreadsheets. Those are just parts of the puzzle.

I define a performance system as the people, places and things around you and, most critically, how they interact. This interaction determines whether your system empowers you to thrive or holds you back.

At its core, high performance is communication with ourselves, each other and the moment. The best systems and leaders make this happen, not by accident but through intentional design.

In the Introduction, I quoted James Clear, saying, 'We do not rise to the level of our goals; we fall to the level of our systems'. Those words bear repeating. In my work, I've seen this truth play out repeatedly. The difference between repeat medallists and those who fall short isn't just talent or effort — it's the quality of the systems they've built.

A repeat Olympic yachting gold medallist once put it perfectly when asked about his competitive edge: *'Wherever I go, I take my system with me. It's my home base'.* His routines, habits and structures travelled with him, reducing the thinking load and allowing him to find flow faster than his competitors.

Systems that communicate clearly, align actions with goals, prioritise simplicity and deliver results are the foundation of consistent, repeatable success.

Let's explore how to move beyond game-capable systems (which deliver occasional wins) to championship-capable systems that sustain excellence over time.

Leadership in the system

What comes to mind when you hear the word *leadership*? A boss? A coach? Someone with a title? Let's rethink that. Leadership isn't titles; it's action. It's how you think, how you act, what you say and how you influence those around you. And in the best performance systems, leading yourself is the most important leadership role you can master. When mastered collectively across your team, it is a key competitive advantage.

The foundation of performance leadership is self-mastery, learning to communicate effectively with yourself, addressing your own blind spots and enabling others to succeed by your example. As renowned self-help author Wayne Dyer said, 'You can't give away what you haven't got'. If you're not thriving, how can you create an environment where others thrive?

Even the best-designed systems falter if the people within them lack the focus, behaviours or mindset to make them work. But the good news is that leadership is a skill, not a fixed trait. It can be learned, practised, refined and improved. Championship-calibre leaders understand that their actions ripple outward, shaping the system's culture, processes and results.

Championship-calibre thinking

To build a championship-level system, you must shift your mindset. Stop waiting for external fixes or hierarchical direction. Performance leadership starts when you take ownership of your role within the system.

Ask yourself:

- *What does my role require of me?*
- *How do I influence the people, places and processes around me?*
- *Where am I, even slightly, a bottleneck in this system?*

This shift from seeing leadership as 'out there' to recognising it as 'in here' is transformative to your personal performance and to those around you (work and home). Championship-calibre leaders don't wait for change to happen; they make it happen by leading themselves and inspiring others. They understand that the success of the system starts with their ability to communicate effectively, set the tone and support alignment. When this level of leadership is role-modelled, the performance of our system shifts and lifts.

The power of progress and iteration

No system is ever perfect, and perfection shouldn't be the goal. Progress is. Perfection is an ideal — an illusion of a final, flawless state that never truly arrives. I have seen many athletes and coaches aim here. I did too. But high performers understand that chasing perfection can be paralysing, while progress, refinement and adaptability drive real success.

Building an effective system involves iteration, refining and improving over time. The highest-calibre leaders remain curious, ask the right questions and make small, consistent changes that compound into significant results.

Remember, championship-level performance isn't a destination; it's a journey. Yes, that's a giant cliché but it is true. By committing to leadership within your system and embracing the principles of simplicity, alignment and well-being you're building the foundation for sustained excellence.

Ask yourself:

- *What's one small action you've been avoiding that could move you — and those around you — closer to championship success?*

Systems thrive when they reach a critical mass of high performers — individuals who lead themselves, master their moments and elevate those around them.

You may have seen Simon Sinek's viral video of a lone dancer at a music festival, moving wildly and uninhibited. At first, he dances alone. Then a second dancer joins him, equally bold. Soon, momentum builds, and within moments, the entire crowd is dancing. This is the power of critical mass. One high performer can spark a movement, but it takes others to create unstoppable momentum.

An island of excellence doesn't thrive in isolation, it needs others committed to the same standard to create a lasting impact.

The next chapter delves into the mindset of the sustained high performer.

CHAPTER 4

THE PERFORMER

Here's a question for you. What makes someone a high performer? Is it their results, their skills or the accolades they've earned?

I remember asking this question of a group of high-performance coaches at a conference. The answer from the floor that got the most nods was 'find a high performing athlete'.

At first glance, it might seem like these external markers define success, but when you look closer, you'll see that high performers are far more than experts in their craft. They are masterful in how they approach their work, manage their decisions and carry themselves every single day, at work and at home. They don't just deliver results; they shape the systems they are part of, influence the people around them and create a legacy that transcends individual achievements and medal counts.

Performance mastery

Let's break it down. Performance mastery is more than technical skill or raw talent. For high performers, mastery unfolds across three dimensions: the self, the moment and the system.

Mastering the self means taking responsibility for your mindset, behaviours and habits. High performers don't leave these to chance. They build routines that amplify what works and ruthlessly eliminate what doesn't. Why? Because distractions cost far more than just time. They drain energy, erode momentum and derail results.

Mastering the moment is clarity under pressure. High performers stay present, adapting to what's in front of them while staying aligned with what matters most. When plans go awry (as they always do) they don't panic. They course-correct with purpose and precision.

Mastering the system requires understanding the people, processes and environments around you and actively working to strengthen them. High performers know that individual success is fleeting without a strong, aligned system to support it. That's why they invest in building trust, alignment and clear communication within their teams.

Think of these dimensions as gears in a finely tuned machine. When they're in sync, they create a powerful, sustainable momentum. When one falters, the whole system suffers.

The clock doesn't stop

Time is the one thing we can't control. But it's not a limitation for high performers; it's a force that brings clarity. The Olympic clock ticks relentlessly, and most athletes have only one or two shots at it. Four years isn't a long time. Every choice either compounds progress or wastes precious energy.

I worked with a cyclist who fell into the trap of chasing every possible gain through new diets, new gear and new training trends. He was busy, but not better. Weeks passed, and real progress stalled. When he finally cut the noise and focused on what truly mattered, his performance took off.

> **The best don't just manage time; they master their focus.**

Time isn't the enemy — it's a partner in solving the performance puzzle. It forces hard questions: *What matters most? Where is my energy best spent?* The best don't just manage time; they master their focus.

Lead by example

My first training camp as a cyclist with the Canadian National Team was eye-opening, not because of the competition, but because of one individual.

Steve Bauer was a yellow jersey winner at the Tour de France and a World and Olympic medallist. His leadership struck me immediately. It wasn't commanding the room or shouting instructions, but how he carried himself.

Steve's professionalism was unwavering. Everything he did, from his preparation to his interactions with teammates, communicated his standards. He didn't just demand excellence; he demonstrated it. His attention to detail, respect for others and dedication to the system set the tone for everyone around him. It was clear that his success was more than talent; it was about the choices he made and the example he set.

This experience shaped my understanding of performance leadership within high performance. It's not enough to excel; you must inspire others through your actions. The greatest high performers lead by example, showing what's possible with focus, discipline and integrity.

Stewardship and legacy

Now, let's go deeper. High performers don't see their work as just their own. They view themselves as stewards of something larger — a team, a system, a legacy. Like the All Blacks, who see their jerseys as symbols of those who came before and those who will come after, high performers understand that their actions today shape opportunities for others tomorrow.

This perspective transforms how they make decisions. They don't act out of ego or short-term gain. Instead, they act with purpose, responsibility and an unwavering commitment to excellence. Their deeper goal is to create a culture of excellence that lasts long after they're gone.

The performer's challenge to you

So, what about you?

Ask yourself:

- *How am I leading myself each day?*
- *Am I mastering the self, the moment and the system I am in?*
- *What legacy am I building through my actions?*

PART ONE: THE WORLD OF HIGH PERFORMANCE

Having explored the performer's mindset, let's now reflect on the concept of the *podium*, which is the process of fulfilment, pride and alignment with who you truly are.

CHAPTER 5

THE PODIUM

What is your podium? Is it a medal? A title? A moment of recognition? Or is it something deeper, like a sense of fulfilment, pride and alignment with who you truly are? Too often, we fixate on the tangible rewards at the end of the journey, forgetting that the true podium is the fulfilment of purpose.

When we think of the podium, it's easy to imagine standing on it, arms raised in triumph. But before that moment comes the climb. A journey filled with decisions, sacrifices and moments of doubt. Purpose drives performance and maintains our momentum in these peaks and troughs.

Find your internal compass

US president John F. Kennedy said, 'Effort and courage are not enough without purpose and direction'. Purpose isn't just a concept, it's the anchor that makes effort meaningful. It's what gives direction to your efforts and meaning to your sacrifices. But let's be honest: purpose can feel abstract, even elusive. How do you find it? How do you know it's real?

Ask yourself:

- *What would make my effort feel meaningful, even if no one else noticed?*

Let that question sit with you. Go beyond impressing others or achieving external validation and align your actions with what truly matters to you.

Mark Twain wrote, 'The two most important days in your life are the day you are born and the day you find out why.' Your purpose is that 'why'. It's the stream that runs beneath everything you do, feeding your actions with clarity and strength. Without it, even the greatest achievements can feel hollow. With it, every step (even the hard ones) becomes a part of something greater.

In a 2017 update of her acclaimed book *Mindset,* Stanford professor Carol Dweck introduces a powerful distinction in a concept she calls 'false growth mindset'. This is where some people strive to *prove* themselves while others strive to *improve*.[3] Purpose is the driving force behind the latter. When you focus on improving rather than proving, you engage with your journey in a way that fuels growth, resilience and fulfilment.

Values guides you

If purpose is the source, then values are the currents that shape its flow. They guide your decisions, helping you navigate life's complexities with integrity and intention. But here's the catch — many people haven't clarified their values. They might say they value 'integrity' or 'excellence', but when asked what those words mean to them personally and how they appear deliberately in their life, they struggle to articulate an answer.

Here's a question to explore: *What do I stand for?* Write it down. Reflect on it. Are your daily actions in alignment with your answer?

Performance leaders don't just identify their values; they live them. They use their values as a lens to make decisions, ensuring that every choice aligns with their deeper purpose.

Performance leaders live their values.

Values are like the threads in a tapestry, weaving meaning and coherence into your actions. When they are clear and consistent, they bring harmony to your efforts. But when values are ignored or misaligned, the result is chaos in your choices and your sense of direction.

Principles are values in action

Let's take this further. If values are the currents, principles are the banks of the river. They are the structures that give shape and direction to your actions. Principles are values in motion. They turn abstract ideas into concrete behaviours. Without them, values can become empty words; with them, values become transformative.

Here's an example. Two people might share the value of 'family', but one person's principles might prioritise loyalty, while another's principles might emphasise open communication. The same value leads to different actions because of differing principles.

What about you? Ask yourself:

- *What principles guide my decisions?*

- *Are they aligned with my values?*
- *Are they serving my purpose?*

Performance leaders are intentional about the principles they uphold, using them as a framework for consistent, purpose-driven action.

Principles ensure that your river stays on course, no matter how turbulent the waters become. They give you the structure to act with confidence and integrity, even under pressure.

On reflection

Let's bring this home. Your podium isn't a destination; it's the alignment of your purpose, values and principles. It's that moment when everything flows together, when your efforts feel not just rewarding but deeply fulfilling. But how do you get there?

Ask yourself:

- *What is my purpose? What is my 'why'?*
- *What are my values? What do I stand for, and are my actions aligned with that?*
- *What are my principles? How do I translate my values into consistent, purposeful action?*

These aren't easy questions, but they're the bedrock of sustained high performance.

The clearer you are on your purpose, the more your values and principles align. And when those three lock together, the podium (whatever that looks like for you) shifts from possibility to inevitability.

Stewardship is the legacy

Here's the final piece. High performers understand that their podium isn't just for them.

Like the New Zealand All Blacks, who see their jerseys as symbols of those who came before and those who will come after, high performers view their success as part of something larger. They see themselves as stewards of their team, their system and their legacy.

> **Create a culture of excellence that outlasts you.**

This perspective changes everything. Beyond your achievement, it's how your actions ripple outward, inspiring and enabling others. Create a culture of excellence that outlasts you. High performers don't just strive for success; they strive to leave things better than they found them.

Choose your podium

So, where do you go from here? Start with the questions. Reflect on your purpose, your values and your principles. Use them to guide your actions, shape your decisions and align your efforts with what truly matters.

Your podium isn't a far-off dream. It's here in the clarity of your purpose, the strength of your values and the consistency of your principles. It's the legacy you build, step by step, through intentional, purpose-driven action.

AMPLIFY

There's more to explore, and your podium — your moment of alignment and fulfilment — is closer than you think.

A podium moment is not enough; *sustaining* high performance requires a relentless dance of adaptation and refinement. Next, we dive into how to keep it all going under changing conditions and pressure.

CHAPTER 6

SUSTAINING HIGH PERFORMANCE

Imagine watching a Cirque du Soleil act, where a performer is balancing on a unicycle, juggling flaming torches and keeping a spinning plate perfectly steady. The audience isn't captivated because they started the act; they're locked in because they're sustaining it — adjusting, adapting and never losing focus.

High performance isn't about reaching the top once. It's about staying there. My obsession became the shift from high performance to sustained high performance — because that's where the real challenge lies. And sustaining it isn't luck; it's systems, leadership and processes coming together repeatedly and deliberately.

> Sustained success is about doing better with less.

We learn the most from repeat medallists, championship-capable teams and businesses that keep winning. They don't rely on one-off moments. They refine, simplify and lock in what works.

Instead of layering on more complexity, they step back and ask, *What really matters?*

Sustained success is about doing better with less. And that takes precision, discipline and clarity.

Redefining excellence

What does excellence mean to you?

High performers don't just aim to beat others or chase external rewards. Their compass is internal. Instead of asking, 'How do I stay ahead of the competition?', they ask, 'What's the best I'm capable of?'

I once worked with an athlete who was preparing for her second Olympics. She already had a medal, but she wasn't satisfied. Her goal was to become the best version of herself at the next Games, not just standing on the podium again. She questioned everything in her preparation, looking for small gaps she could close and ways to refine her mindset, her recovery and her technique.

Excellence is a moving target.

Unlike her first Olympics, in her second Games she wasn't competing against anyone else. Her biggest rival was her own potential. When the Games came, the medal she earned was proof of her relentless commitment to performance leadership. The medal was awarded because of what she learned about how to earn it.

The truth is that excellence is a moving target. It's not something you achieve and hold onto — it's something you sustain by evolving, adapting and pushing beyond what you thought possible. Sustained high performance is more than asking, *'What's next?'* It's about constantly assessing, *'What must I refine, reinforce or rethink to stay ahead?'* The best don't just chase the future; they sharpen the present.

Sweeping the sheds

There's a story from one of the most successful teams in history, the New Zealand All Blacks rugby team, that always sticks with me. They have a ritual called 'sweeping the sheds', which involves senior players cleaning the locker room after every match. As James Kerr describes in *Legacy: What the All Blacks Can Teach Us About the Business of Life*, this practice is practical, not symbolic.[4] It shows humility, respect and accountability. It says, 'No one is above the team'.

Sustained performance is the culture you create and role model, and it goes beyond talent or hard work. The All Blacks' legacy is measured more by the ethos they've built than by their wins. Their culture inspires excellence across generations. True greatness comes from the habits and values you cultivate and pass on.

> **Sustained performance goes beyond talent or hard work.**

So, what's your equivalent of sweeping the sheds? How do you keep yourself grounded, focused and ready for the next challenge? Sustaining high performance means creating habits and systems that endure. They remind you why you started and where you came from to keep you moving forward.

Your commitment to sustained high performance

Sustaining high performance is a daily choice. It requires asking yourself some questions that matter and having the courage to act on the answers.

Let's replay a few here:

Are you clear on your purpose and values? Are they guiding your decisions?

Are you focusing on the few critical actions that truly matter?

Are you learning and adapting, using every success and setback to refine your approach?

This work isn't easy, but it's worth it. Sustaining high performance requires persistence, curiosity and humility. You commit to growth and refinement every single day. The rewards for yourself and those you lead are immeasurable.

PART ONE SUMMARY

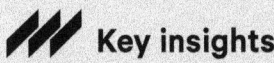 **Key insights**

High performance isn't about doing more — it's about focusing on *less but better*. The best performers master key literacies.

Problem literacy — Identifying and focusing on the *right* problems. Not every challenge is worth solving. Elite performers cut through distractions and prioritise what truly matters.

Preparation literacy — Success isn't last-minute effort; it's built on strong systems, habits and routines. Champions invest in foundational preparation that makes high performance inevitable.

Performance literacy — Knowing is not enough; execution under pressure is what sets high performers apart. The best don't rise to the occasion — they fall to the level of their preparation.

Leadership in high performance — Leadership is about action, not titles. High performers take ownership of their role, lead by example and influence the system around them.

The podium as a process — True success isn't just external achievement. It's alignment between purpose, values and principles. Sustained performance comes from clarity, consistency and legacy.

Sustaining high performance — Reaching the top is one thing; staying there is another. The best simplify, refine and adapt to keep winning over time.

Common blind spots

Even the best fall into traps that limit growth.

Chasing every opportunity — High performers don't do *everything*, they do *what matters most*.

Mistaking busyness for progress — More effort doesn't always mean better results. Precision beats exhaustion.

Ignoring system weaknesses — Talent alone isn't enough. High performance is sustained by strong systems, not just individuals.

Amplifying questions

1. *Am I solving the right problems, or just the most urgent ones?*
2. *Is my preparation making success inevitable, or am I relying on last-minute effort?*
3. *Do I have a system that ensures I can deliver under pressure, not just when things go smoothly?*

PART TWO

THE FOUNDATIONS OF HIGH PERFORMANCE

AMPLIFY

Having examined the world of high performance, we now focus on the *practical steps* to build and sustain it.

In the following chapters, you'll explore how personal experience (both triumphs and setbacks) shapes essence, how daily habits feed into excellence and how empowerment multiplies impact. You'll also learn about reframing challenges into catalysts for growth.

CHAPTER 7

YOUR GAME OF EXPERIENCE, ESSENCE, EXCELLENCE AND EMPOWERMENT

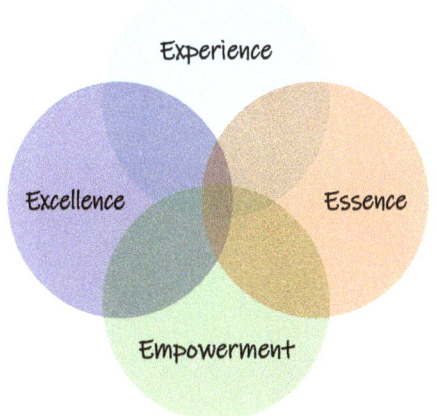

What has brought you to this moment in your life, your career and your journey? High performance is discovering and building on your blueprint. It's deeply personal and profoundly connected to who you are. That's where your game begins, with the unique combination of your experiences, your essence, your pursuit of excellence and your empowerment.

Experience is your journey so far

Think of your experiences as the building blocks of your performance. Every victory, every setback and every lesson is the raw material you bring to the table. As an expert leader once told me after a traumatic loss in life, 'It is vital to pay attention to what you are learning'. It is how we translate experience into our essence, excellence and empowerment, no matter what.

I work with many leaders who face tough challenges and high pressure. Recently, one leader described their experiences as burdens, moments they wished they could erase. Over time, they began to dig deeper into them for insights. They realised those challenges had sharpened their judgement, taught them resilience and given them a perspective others lacked. That's the power of experience. Win or lose, it shapes your ability to see patterns, anticipate challenges and respond under pressure.

Experience is only as valuable as your ability to reflect on it.

Ask yourself:

- *What have I learned from my journey so far?*
- *How can those lessons guide me now?*

High performers don't just live through experiences; they extract the wisdom they hold.

Essence is your core identity

Your essence is who you are. It includes the values you hold, the purpose that drives you and the energy you bring to everything you do. It's your anchor, especially when the stakes are high and the pressure is on. Without clarity around your essence, it's easy to get pulled in a hundred different directions, losing sight of what truly matters.

Think of your essence as the keel of a boat. It keeps you stable, no matter how rough the waters get. High performers who understand their essence make decisions with confidence and authenticity. They're not swayed by every passing trend or external pressure because they know what they stand for.

What grounds you? What values guide your decisions? These aren't small questions, but they're worth sitting with. When you're connected to your essence, you move through the world with clarity and strength. Rather than pursuing perfection, you're seeking alignment and being true to who you are.

Excellence is your standard for growth

Excellence is not a competition with anyone else.

I watched one particular athlete training for an international competition. Every detail mattered to them. But what struck me wasn't their skill; it was their commitment. They approached every session with the mindset of *How can I improve today?* That's excellence. It's a daily practice.

Ask yourself:

- *What does excellence mean to me?*

Beyond grand gestures or big wins, excellence is the small, consistent actions that add up over time. It is consistently choosing 'improving' over 'proving' even when no one's watching.

Empowerment moves from me to we

Here's where it all comes together. Empowerment isn't just about you; it's how you use your strengths to lift others. Sustained high performance doesn't happen in isolation. It's something we create together in teams, families and organisations.

Empowerment shifts the focus from 'me' to 'we' by creating an environment where everyone can thrive and where your strengths amplify those around you. I've seen this ripple effect in action countless times. When one person steps into their power, it inspires others to do the same.

So, let me ask: *Who do you empower? How do you create space for others to succeed?*

True high performance is more than achieving your own goals; you are contributing to something bigger than yourself.

Build your foundation

These four areas of experience, essence, excellence and empowerment are the foundation of your game. They're interconnected, each strengthening the others. Your experiences shape your essence, your essence fuels your pursuit of excellence and your excellence drives your ability to empower others.

As you reflect on these areas, consider how they show up in your life.

PART TWO: THE FOUNDATIONS OF HIGH PERFORMANCE

Ask yourself:

- *How does my journey inform my decisions?*
- *How do my values anchor me?*
- *What standard am I setting for myself?*
- *How am I using my strengths to make an impact?*

Sustained high performance is a puzzle, but it isn't a mystery. It involves doing the work to build a foundation that lasts. And it starts with you. Let's take the first step together.

Next, we'll see how *awareness* helps you harness doubts, maintain focus and keep your system flourishing.

CHAPTER 8

AWARENESS AND ITS BLACK ARROW

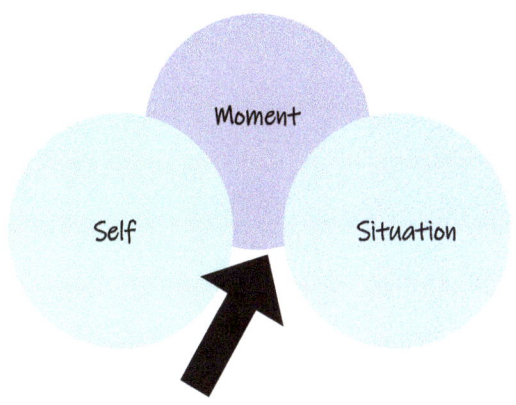

Ignore the Black Arrow at your peril

A swimmer stood at the edge of the pool, the scent of chlorine thick in the air, the muffled echoes of splashing water surrounding her. Her hands flexed at her sides, her breath shallow, her mind racing ahead of the moment. '*Am I ready for this?*', she wondered.

Her coach leaned in, voice steady. *'Trust the water. Trust your training. Just swim.'*

Something shifted. A deep breath. A steadying exhale. The noise in her head didn't disappear — but it lost its grip. She wasn't pushing doubt away; she was choosing a different thought. *You've done the work. Let it flow.*

When the buzzer sounded, she exploded off the blocks — not in search of perfection, but in full command of the moment.

This is the quiet battle of high performance. Not just knowing the plan, but managing the inner resistance — the nagging voice that questions, hesitates, distracts. I call it the Black Arrow of Awareness. It's the whisper at the worst possible time: *What if I fail? What if I'm not ready?*

Everyone faces it, whether on the field, in a meeting or in the middle of an ordinary day. Left unchecked, it saps energy and steals focus. But here's the real skill — the best don't waste time fighting the first thought. They master the second.

The power of the second thought

Swiss psychologist Carl Jung believed that the human mind is shaped as much by what we choose to notice as by what we suppress. The Black Arrow (our first, unconscious thought) is part of the human condition. It's not something we can eliminate entirely, nor should we try. As Jung suggested, 'We cannot change anything until we accept it'. What matters most is what comes next: the second thought. That's where we regain our power.

> **'We cannot change anything until we accept it.'**

This insight is echoed in addiction recovery. Those who thrive in recovery don't necessarily eliminate their initial cravings or doubts. Instead, they learn to notice them, acknowledge them without judgement, and redirect their energy toward a healthier choice. The Black Arrow is never fully eradicated; it's managed, one second thought at a time. This practice transforms vulnerability into strength.

Self-awareness starts from within

Self-awareness is the foundation for navigating the Black Arrow. It's the ability to notice your inner dialogue, recognise your triggers and understand the habits that influence your decisions. Daniel Kahneman notes in *Thinking, Fast and Slow* that our minds are wired for shortcuts, which can be both a strength and a vulnerability.[5] Self-awareness sharpens our ability to discern between helpful instincts and unhelpful patterns.

I often ask the people I work with, *What's the story you're telling yourself right now?* This simple question has an incredible way of surfacing the Black Arrow bringing it fully visible to empower us to shift the narrative.

Focus on the now

Moment awareness is about being fully present. When distractions and doubts arise, staying in the moment can feel like balancing on a tightrope. Ceri Evans explains in *Perform Under Pressure* that high performers don't ignore the noise — they learn to work within it.[6] They focus on what they can control and let the rest fade into the background.

In the military, fear is ever-present. A soldier standing at the edge of a battlefield doesn't have the luxury of eliminating it. In training, they're taught not to suppress fear but to step forward *with* it

— to let it be there, acknowledge it and still take action. One veteran described it to me this way: *'Courage isn't the absence of fear. It's knowing fear is in the room with you and stepping through the door anyway'.*

I once spoke with a police SWAT team leader who described the first time he had to breach a door, knowing danger waited on the other side. His hands were steady, but his mind screamed with every possible outcome. His training gave him the tools to move despite the fear. *One step. One breath. One task at a time.* And in that moment, action took over.

> **The presence of doubt doesn't diminish our ability to act.**

One Olympic coach I worked with captured this beautifully, saying *'It's not about erasing the fear. It's letting it sit in the corner while you do your work.'* This reframing is incredibly powerful. It reminds us that the presence of doubt doesn't diminish our ability to act. It's a companion to the moment, but doesn't have to take control.

Situational awareness is seeing the field

Situational awareness expands the lens beyond the self and the moment. You understand your environment, your team and the broader context. In *The Chimp Paradox*, Steve Peters highlights how managing our reactive mind (the 'chimp') allows us to see situations with clarity rather than through the lens of fear or frustration.[7]

A high performer with strong situational awareness thinks beyond their role, to consider how their actions align with the bigger picture. This ability to see both the trees and the forest separates good decision-makers from great ones.

Acknowledge without judgement

Here's a core truth: the Black Arrow is not your enemy. It's simply a signal, one you can use to your advantage. The most resilient performers don't fight it. They notice it, name it and let it pass. Choosing a second thought takes courage but changes the result every time.

When the Black Arrow strikes, ask yourself:

- *What is this thought telling me?*
- *Is it helpful or just noise?*
- *What's the second thought I want to hold onto?*

The dragon protects the gold

The Black Arrow feels intimidating because it guards something valuable. Yet I often say, *'The dragon protects the gold'.* Your doubts and fears don't appear randomly — they show up when you're close to something meaningful. Instead of fearing the Black Arrow, recognise it as a sign that you're stepping into your potential.

I see this every time my daughters step onto the stage to sing. No matter how many performances they've done, the nerves always show up. My younger daughter Emmy once admitted she hated the feeling of that flutter in her stomach that made her doubt if she was ready. Before one show, my older daughter Gracie turned to her and said, *'Don't worry, the butterflies in our tummy are getting us ready'.*

The nerves weren't a problem to solve or an obstacle to overcome. They were part of the process — proof that something important was about to happen.

One Olympic coach I worked with had a reframing mantra for their athletes: *'The fear you feel means you're ready'.* That small shift reframed the Black Arrow from a barrier to a guide. The key wasn't in eliminating fear — it was in acknowledging it without letting it decide the next move.

Putting awareness into practice

Awareness is a daily practice. The next time you face a challenge, remember these steps:

1. **Notice the Black Arrow** — Pause and name the first thought.
2. **Shift to the second thought** — Choose a narrative grounded in your preparation and values.
3. **Engage with the moment** — Stay present and focus on what matters most.
4. **Expand your view** — Look at the bigger picture and align your actions accordingly.

The ability to navigate the Black Arrow isn't just for Olympians or leaders. It's for anyone striving to live with clarity and purpose. By cultivating awareness, we unlock the capacity to meet challenges with resilience, grace and focus.

PART TWO: THE FOUNDATIONS OF HIGH PERFORMANCE

With greater awareness, you gain perspective. In the next chapter, we'll discuss the Three Lights of performance leadership — floodlight, spotlight and greenlight — which are essential for leading with adaptability and clarity.

CHAPTER 9

THE THREE LIGHTS OF LEADERSHIP

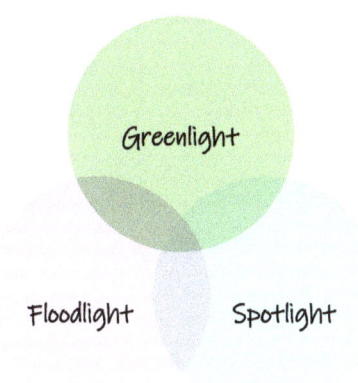

Leadership doesn't mean having all the answers or holding a single perspective. It's knowing when to zoom out, when to focus in and when to act decisively. I imagine it as using three different kinds of light: the floodlight, the spotlight and the greenlight. Together, they create clarity, focus and momentum and are essential tools for navigating high-performance environments.

Let's explore how mastering these lights can transform your ability to lead, adapt and thrive.

The floodlight sees the bigger picture

Imagine you're in a theatre. The lights dim, the stage comes alive and the floodlights illuminate everything — not just the lead actors but the entire scene. You see the relationships, the movements, the patterns that make the performance work.

This is the floodlight perspective in leadership — the ability to step back, take in the bigger picture and anticipate what's coming next. It's beyond the immediate game, race or quarter. It's about thinking in layers, understanding long-term shifts and positioning yourself to adapt before the change happens.

Arie de Geus, in *The Living Company*, studied businesses that lasted for centuries while others faded in decades.[8] What set them apart? Their ability to learn and adapt faster than the competition, using a floodlight perspective to spot trends, anticipate industry shifts and evolve before they were forced to.

I've seen the same principle in elite sport. A gold medal-winning Olympic leader once told me, *'We don't just plan for the next match — we plan for how the game is changing.'* In their high-performance system, the floodlight was always on, scanning for shifts in tactics, training science and even cultural changes that could impact the team's future success.

The same is true in Olympic talent development. If we only focus on the next Games we miss the athletes who could dominate in eight or 12 years. The best Olympic systems train for the next event while developing for the next two to three Olympic cycles.

The floodlight perspective is about seeing. But, most importantly, it's about understanding context. It allows leaders to spot patterns, anticipate challenges and shape the future rather than react to it. Whether in sport, business or life, those who master this approach set the pace.

The spotlight focuses when it matters most

While the floodlight gives breadth, the spotlight brings precision. Think back to the theatre where the scene changes, and suddenly, the spotlight narrows on a single actor. The rest of the stage fades, and your attention is drawn to the critical moment. In leadership, the spotlight helps you focus on what matters most, cutting through distractions.

I worked with an executive navigating a major corporate merger. The integration process was chaotic, and his team was overwhelmed by competing priorities. His instinct was to address every issue, but the constant firefighting drained the team's energy.

> **While the floodlight gives breadth, the spotlight brings precision.**

We discussed shifting to a spotlight approach, so I asked, 'What's the one thing your team needs to focus on right now?' After reflecting, he decided that aligning the sales teams was the priority. That clarity allowed his team to direct their energy effectively to the main thing in their world, creating momentum and reducing stress.

I was working with an Olympic sailing coach in Europe who was frustrated by the constant rule changes and shifting conditions in the sport. Her sailors were overwhelmed by trying to process everything at once and struggling to focus on the race ahead.

One day, she called a team meeting and laid it out simply: *'You're here to sail. That's it.'*

She told them, *'I'll take care of the floodlight — the shifting rules, the big picture, the things out of your control. You take care of the spotlight — your technique, your decisions, your race.'*

With that clarity, the team stopped worrying about the uncontrollable and started executing what they did best. And when the competition came, they were ready, not distracted. They were focused, knowing that their job was simply to sail.

Using the spotlight moves us from deciding what to focus on, to having the courage to let go of the rest. This ability to focus, even in the midst of chaos, is what drives results in high-stakes environments.

The greenlight moves us to decisive action

Floodlight and spotlight provide clarity and focus, but the greenlight represents something deeper: the courage to take action when it matters most. In leadership, the defining moment is where insight turns into impact, and the choice to commit overrides hesitation.

> **The defining moment is where insight turns into impact.**

The greenlight teaches us that waiting for perfect conditions is a luxury. In high-performance environments, perfection is often a mirage. Instead, great leaders lean into the unknown, trusting in their preparation, their team and their ability to adapt.

Daniel Kahneman explains in *Thinking, Fast and Slow* that our brains constantly juggle fast, instinctive decisions with slow, deliberate analysis.[9] The greenlight is where these come together and the ability to act decisively is informed by instinct and reason.

The next time you face a critical decision, ask yourself:

- *What's holding me back?*
- *What have I already done to prepare for this moment?*

Often, the real obstacle isn't the situation; it's the fear of moving forward. When you trust the work you've put in and take that step, you'll find that action is often the catalyst for clarity.

It reminds me of the story of two doors in heaven. One says 'Heaven' and has no queue. The other says 'Lecture on Heaven' and has the biggest line you've ever seen. Most people wait, thinking they need more certainty before stepping through. But high performers don't stand in line for more information — they walk through the door.

You don't need to know all the answers. Courage allows you to go, even when the path isn't fully lit. That's the power of the greenlight. It creates momentum, builds confidence and moves you closer to your goals.

Move seamlessly between the lights

The real skill isn't simply knowing what each light represents. Rather, it is the ability to transition seamlessly between them, like an orchestra conductor moving her attention between players, but keeping the view of the full score and lifting specific sections or individuals just at the right time to craft a harmonious performance.

An Olympic team leader I worked with faced a decision of where to shift the lights. The floodlight revealed that a strategic player change was needed to counter an unexpected substitution from the other team. The spotlight narrowed in on a key athlete who was out of sync. Then came the greenlight — a decisive lineup change for the final push.

That call secured their place on the podium. Great leaders know when to step back, when to zoom in and when to commit.

Bringing it all together

When you're faced with a challenge, ask yourself:

- *Am I seeing the bigger picture? What patterns or trends might I be missing? (That's the floodlight.)*
- *Am I focusing on the most critical detail right now? What deserves my attention? (That's the spotlight.)*
- *Is it time to act? What's the decision that will create momentum? (That's the greenlight.)*

Leadership is navigating complexity with purpose and often without perfect clarity. By mastering these three lights, you'll make better decisions and inspire those around you to do the same.

So, the next time you're in a pivotal moment, think about these lights. Use the floodlight to step back, the spotlight to focus in and the green light to move forward. It's a rhythm you can master, that will guide you to sustained high performance.

Next, we connect perspective to purpose, which is the guiding engine that keeps you focused on meaningful efforts, not just urgent tasks.

CHAPTER 10

THE ENGINE OF EXCELLENCE

Purpose, as we explored earlier, is the invisible force that pulls us forward. It enables leaders to harness their experience, express their essence, refine their excellence and empower those around them. It's what transforms potential into reality and gives every action depth and meaning. Without purpose, even the most talented individuals and teams falter. But with it, you unlock something extraordinary — a sense of conviction that fuels high performance, resilience and unity.

> **Purpose is the anchor for everything that matters.**

Purpose is the anchor for everything that matters. It sharpens focus, aligns effort and connects people to a shared mission.

Leaders who understand this don't just motivate their teams; they create systems where purpose drives every decision and interaction. It becomes the heartbeat of a team, the thread that links individual efforts into something far greater.

Purpose in action

Imagine standing at the edge of a dense forest with no map. The trees are endless, and the paths ahead seem infinite. Purpose is the compass that gives direction by aligning you with your true north. It's the difference in performance leadership between motion and progress.

> **Purpose is the compass that gives direction.**

The All Blacks' haka is a perfect example. It's far more than a pre-match ritual. Every movement, every word, is a reminder of who they are, what they stand for and who they represent. Their high-performance manager once explained to me, *'The haka isn't for show. It's a promise to each other, to our history and to the game itself. It connects us to something unbreakable.'* This purpose isn't confined to game day. It's reflected in how they train, the standards they hold each other to and the respect they show for their heritage. Every decision, from strategy to team selection, is filtered through this lens of collective commitment.

The heart of sustained high performance

Purpose turns confidence into conviction and individual effort into collective strength. It transforms a job into a calling, a group into a team and an effort into a legacy. When purpose is clear, it binds people to each other and to the mission in a way that no speech or strategy ever could. It creates a shared understanding that every effort, every setback and every triumph is part of something greater.

The best leaders inspire a relationship with purpose. Instead of merely understanding it, the best move themselves and others into living it. They role model this to help their teams see, feel and believe in it. It becomes a thread that runs through every decision, every action and every interaction. One Olympic coach told me, 'Our purpose gets us all out of bed with a leap'.

Like the map in the forest when you know your purpose, it becomes the compass that guides you through uncertainty and the fuel of progress.

Reflecting on purpose

Take a few minutes to reflect on your purpose. Ask yourself:

- *What energises me, even on the hardest days?*
- *How does my work connect to something bigger than myself?*
- *When have I felt most aligned with my purpose? What was different about those moments?*

Purpose is clarity. Purpose is energy. Purpose brings excellence to life.

So, what's your purpose? Find it, live it and let it guide you to something extraordinary.

Purpose alone isn't enough if the team doesn't *fit*. Next, we explore 'fit-ness', ensuring the group's dynamic fosters true collaboration and collective performance.

CHAPTER 11

FIT-NESS FOR EMPOWERMENT

The key to connection and empowerment

In the quest for excellence, whether in sport, business or personal life, one factor often missed is the concept of fit-ness. That's not physical fitness, it's how well a group fits together. Sustained high performance is never a solo endeavour. It is forged through connection, cohesion and empowerment. When a team truly fits, they achieve a flow state that allows them to jam like a great band, improvising, innovating and adapting to whatever challenges come their way. They find the sweet spot where their approach is both reliable and dynamic, where trust is implicit and where the group performs as one.

In evolutionary theory, the term 'survival of the fittest' is often misunderstood. Far from being the strongest or most aggressive, Herbert Spencer, who coined the phrase, and Charles Darwin would agree that 'fittest' refers to being best adapted to the environment. For teams, fit-ness is about how the pieces come together, how they adapt to their surroundings and how well they function as a cohesive unit. It's not the strongest individual that ensures success, it's the ability of the group to read each other, read the room and flow together.

The shift from 'me' to 'we'

Every championship-calibre team I've worked with has demonstrated this principle. They integrate raw talent or skill into a system that thrives under pressure.

In Chapter Nine I mentioned that Arie de Geus studied why some companies last for centuries while others fail in decades.[10] His research found that long-lasting organisations excelled because they treated themselves as living organisms capable of learning, adapting and evolving. De Geus noted that these organisations prioritise fit-ness by being sensitive to their environment, cohesive in identity and tolerant of diverse perspectives. This adaptability allows them to innovate and sustain success over the long term.

> **The shift from 'me' to 'we' is fundamental.**

The shift from 'me' to 'we' is fundamental to creating systemic fit-ness. Teams that excel in sustained performance function as a united system, not just a collection of high-performing individuals. Consider the recruitment process. Do we hire the most skilled candidate or the one who fits best with the team? In sport and business alike, prioritising team fit-ness (connection and cohesion) over fitness (strengths and endurance) changes the entire dynamic.

Fit-ness in action

I've seen countless high-performance scenarios where a struggling team had all the talent in the world but lacked cohesion. The difference happens when one leader steps in and focuses not on individual abilities but on how the team communicates and collaborates. Fostering trust and alignment transforms the team, delivering results far beyond what their raw talent suggested was possible.

This principle applies just as much in the workplace. When hiring a new analyst for the New Zealand Olympic teams, I encountered a candidate who, on paper, was exceptional. She spoke multiple languages, held advanced degrees and ran her own business. But when asked to describe a turning point in her life where she had failed and learned, her response was, 'I've never failed'. This was a red flag. In sport, failure is part of the game.

> In sport, failure is part of the game.

Teams must learn, adapt and grow from setbacks. Without that experience of learning from loss, fitting into a high-performance environment becomes a challenge. Fit-ness accelerates us to alignment and adaptability.

The fit-ness of sustained high performance

Teams that prioritise fit-ness build a shared identity that fosters trust, cohesion and resilience. They create environments where collaboration thrives and individuals feel empowered to bring their best and can sustain excellence over the long game. A cohesive team doesn't just survive uncertainty; it thrives in it, improvising and innovating like a band hitting all the right notes, creating something far greater than the sum of its parts.

Systemic fit-ness allows teams to adapt to the environment, align individual strengths for collective success and build teams that are greater than any individual could ever be alone. When leaders master the art of creating fit-ness, they empower teams to reach their fullest potential. They cultivate trust, alignment and a sense of belonging to something bigger than themselves.

Fit-ness isn't just a tool. It's the foundation of connection, empowerment and enduring success. The question moves from, 'Do you fit?' to 'How can we fit together better?' That's where empowerment begins and where lasting legacies are built.

With fit-ness in place, the stage is set for mastery. Next, we delve into the deeper territory beyond expertise into true craft mastery that reshapes how you and your team operate.

CHAPTER 12

CRAFT MASTERY

There's a difference between knowing and truly understanding; between executing a skill and embodying a craft. Mastery is more about transcending expertise than accumulating it. It is the difference that I see often between a knowledge expert and a performance expert. One knows 'what', but the other knows 'how' and does it.

It's the subtle, instinctive competence that comes when knowledge, experience and self-awareness align. Those who pursue mastery are more than just practitioners of their field. They are leaders of performance and architects of sustained excellence.

> **Competence comes when knowledge, experience and self-awareness align.**

The journey from novice to expert is well-documented. Building on the widely accepted Dreyfus model of skill acquisition, Patricia Benner, the renowned nurse educator, described how learners progress through five stages: novice, advanced beginner, competent, proficient and expert.[11] Novices rely on rules and guidelines to function. Experts, on the other hand, see patterns, anticipate outcomes and act fluidly.

But what lies beyond expertise? It's the elusive territory of mastery, where experience sharpens intuition and blind spots are deliberately confronted. Masters don't just perform; they elevate others and reshape their craft.

The novice to expert continuum

Let's break it down. A novice begins by memorising and applying rules, often feeling overwhelmed by complexity. With time and guidance, they become an advanced beginner, spotting familiar contexts but still dependent on external direction. At the competent stage, they gain a sense of control, planning actions and making deliberate decisions. By the time they're proficient, they no longer deliberate over every move; intuition starts to emerge.

> **True masters go beyond instinct to reflect, refine and grow.**

Experts take this one step further. They operate instinctively, recognising patterns in their environment almost without thinking. As Benner observed in clinical nursing professionals, experts can 'see the whole' and make decisions faster and with greater precision than their less-experienced counterparts. Yet expertise is not the finish line. True masters go beyond acting on instinct to reflect, refine and grow. They seek feedback, challenge their assumptions and pursue depth over breadth.

Mastery is the art of the next step

Here's where the leap to mastery occurs. Mastery involves the deliberate practice of reducing blind spots. Stuart Dreyfus himself once told me, 'Masters have fewer blind spots because they see themselves as learners, not finishers'. Masters don't merely operate at the edge of their comfort zone; they expand it by questioning their methods and decisions, even when those methods are successful.

It's a mindset shift from *'What works now?'* to *'What could work better?'*

> **Masters understand that their craft is dynamic, not static.**

Masters understand that their craft is dynamic, not static. That's the difference between expertise and mastery. Experts perform at a high level. Masters redefine what high performance looks like.

The masterful coach

I knew one particular Olympic coach who embodied this idea. She'd repeatedly led athletes to the podium, yet she constantly sought to refine her craft. 'Winning is a moment', she told me. 'Sustaining high performance is a lifetime.' Her expertise was undeniable, but she remained open to learning by attending workshops, collaborating with specialists in unrelated fields and analysing what worked and why it worked.

One year, she faced a challenge that would test everything she knew — preparing a team for an event where the competition had evolved faster than expected. The tactics that had once delivered success were now being countered, and relying on the old playbook would no longer be enough.

Instead of doubling down on past methods, she did what true masters do — she questioned what she knew and expanded her learning. She spent time studying emerging trends, speaking with coaches in completely different sports and breaking down performance in ways she never had before. She even brought in military strategists to refine decision-making under pressure, challenging her team to think and adapt at speed.

By competition day, her athletes were ahead of the game. While their rivals stuck to familiar strategies, her team anticipated and adapted in real time, turning uncertainty into an advantage. They didn't just win — they changed the way their sport was played.

This was mastery at work. The ability to stay ahead by staying open, evolving faster than the environment and recognising that greatness isn't about what you know, it's about how willing you are to learn.

The master carpenter

A great friend of mine is a master carpenter. He has spent decades honing his craft. Their tools feel like extensions of their hands, and their movements seem effortless. But what makes him truly remarkable is more than his skill with wood; it's his understanding of the material. He knows how each grain will respond to pressure, how to balance precision with flexibility and when to adapt the design to suit the wood rather than force the wood to fit the design.

Now, compare this to a novice with a manual. The novice can follow instructions and perhaps create a serviceable table. But the master creates something extraordinary with a piece that tells a story, that feels timeless. That's because the master does more than just apply knowledge — they adapt it, evolve it and bring something deeper to the process. They don't simply *know* the craft; they *are* the craft.

Mastery and performance leadership

Mastery is the defining trait of high-performance leadership in any field. True masters go beyond their own growth; they create systems and cultures that elevate others, ensuring that excellence isn't just achieved, but sustained.

The path to mastery isn't easy, but it's what separates those who maintain success from those who advance it. It takes humility to question what you know, curiosity to explore what you don't and the willingness to embrace discomfort as a teacher. Masters don't see setbacks as failures — they see them as fuel for refinement.

Ask yourself:

- *Where am I on the novice-to-master continuum?*
- *Am I still relying on rules, or am I ready to navigate the unknown?*
- *Have I settled for expertise, or am I truly pursuing mastery?*

Mastery is more than skill — it's about presence, impact and the energy that lifts others. Next, we'll explore how this intangible force — mana — resonates through teams and transforms leadership.

CHAPTER 13

MANA

Leadership is actions and words and also deeply sensed energy: a presence that lasts after you've left the room. The concept exists across cultures. It's *chi* in Chinese philosophy, *prana* in Indian traditions and the Western idea of *gravitas*. Here in New Zealand, we call it *mana*, from Polynesian culture.

A blend of authenticity, connection and impact, it is the life force we all carry and what performance leaders maximise. Mana isn't something you declare or impose. It's the force others feel when your leadership is grounded in clarity, trust and purpose. Think of it as the resonant note that hangs in the air after a bell is struck.

Mana reflects the harmony between your internal essence and the way you engage with the world. It's your values in action, your authenticity felt in every decision and your conviction resonating with those you lead. When leaders cultivate mana, they create ripples that inspire teams, build trust and sustain high performance.

Mana in action

A senior leader I worked with was preparing their team for a transformative change. The stakes were high, and the team was nervous. This leader didn't begin with grand strategies or a motivational speech. Instead, they shared a personal story about when they had faced uncertainty and how they stayed true to their values. The room shifted not because of the story, but because of the authenticity behind it. The leader's mana filled the space, creating trust and anchoring the team in a shared sense of purpose.

Itzhak Perlman, the world-renowned violinist, faced an extraordinary challenge during a concert. Stricken with polio as a child, he walked onto the stage with leg braces and crutches, a painstaking process the audience was familiar with. But one evening, something unexpected happened. A string on his violin snapped just as he began to play. Instead of stopping or asking for help, he paused, closed his eyes, and signalled the conductor to begin again. He adapted, playing a symphony with only three strings. The result was breathtaking because of the sheer presence and mastery he brought to the moment. Perlman's music and mana filled the room that night, leaving the audience in awe. He later said, 'Sometimes it is the artist's task to find out how much music you can still make with what you have left.'

Mana is not loud or flashy. It's felt in the quiet confidence of someone who knows their values, their essence and lives by them. It's the reason people lean in to listen, follow willingly and feel empowered to step into their own potential.

PART TWO: THE FOUNDATIONS OF HIGH PERFORMANCE

Cultivating mana

Mana doesn't come from knowledge alone. It's the result of alignment between what you believe, what you know and how you act. Leaders with mana understand that their presence speaks before their words do. Their values, behaviours and energy create an unspoken message of integrity and trust.

How do you cultivate mana? Ask yourself:

- *What values guide your leadership? Are they visible in your actions?*
- *How do you create a sense of belonging and purpose for those you lead?*
- *What kind of energy do you bring into a room? How does it impact others?*

The power of vulnerability

One of the most profound sources of mana is vulnerability. Brené Brown reminds us that vulnerability is not a weakness but a strength.[12] Leaders who acknowledge their fears, doubts or mistakes show others that it's OK to be human. This openness doesn't diminish their authority; it amplifies it through their authenticity.

I worked with an Olympic coach who faced immense pressure to deliver results. Instead of masking their challenges, they openly discussed the obstacles with their team and sought their input. This vulnerability strengthened the coach's position and deepened the team's respect and commitment. The team knew they were part of a shared journey, not just delivering someone else's plan. That's mana in action, transforming vulnerability into strength.

The call to mana

Cultivating your mana is a decision. It means aligning your values with your actions, showing fully human authenticity and creating space for others to step into their potential. It's presence, not perfection. When you lead with mana, you go beyond just achieving goals to creating environments where excellence thrives, trust deepens and impact lasts.

Ask yourself:

- *What does my leadership energy say before I speak?*
- *How do I align my values, knowledge and actions to inspire trust and connection?*
- *What legacy of impact am I building through my presence and leadership?*

I have seen many leaders shift to lead with their mana. Their influence resonates far beyond the moment, creating ripples of trust, empowerment and sustained high performance.

Whether you call it mana or presence, the next chapter takes a very practical lens: the '10% Principle'. Focusing on the vital few can multiply your impact exponentially.

CHAPTER 14

THE POWER OF 10%

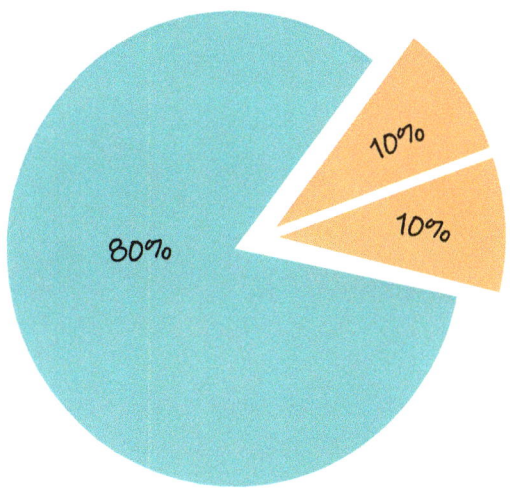

Have you ever felt like you're juggling too many priorities, yet nothing seems to move the needle? That's the paradox many leaders and teams face. The truth is that not everything matters equally. Most of what we do doesn't make a significant difference.

That's where the 10% Principle comes in. It's a powerful framework rooted in focus, alignment and compounding effort that drives sustained success.

The 10% Principle is grounded in the well-known Pareto Principle, which suggests that 80% of outcomes come from 20% of efforts.

But in high-performance environments, the stakes demand even more precision. The best leaders and teams go further, narrowing their attention to the 10% that truly drives results. This means working smarter, not harder. As Dan Sullivan and Benjamin Hardy explore in *10x Is Easier Than 2x*, achieving transformational growth requires a radical shift in focus.[13] It's not about doubling down on everything; rather, identifying and protecting the few things that matter most.

The compound effect of clarity

Think of the 10% as the foundation of a championship-calibre system. When you prioritise these critical areas, every decision, action and resource aligns to amplify the impact. The result? A compounding effect that turns incremental progress into extraordinary outcomes.

One medal-winning team I worked with exemplified this perfectly. They identified their 10% as three core areas: physical conditioning, tactical decision-making and equipment innovation. Every solution they pursued strengthened one of these priorities. Gains in conditioning boosted performance, which enhanced tactical execution, which in turn made better use of their cutting-edge equipment. These interconnected improvements created a ripple effect, driving exponential success. By contrast, teams without clarity spread their energy too thin, chasing marginal gains in too many directions and missing the chance to make meaningful progress.

This principle applies far beyond sport. Consider the business leader navigating a major organisational transformation. Instead of trying to address every challenge, they ask: 'What are the three things that, if done well, will make the biggest difference?' By aligning the team's efforts around those priorities, they achieve their goals and build momentum and resilience along the way.

Protect your 10%

Identifying your 10% is one thing; protecting it is another. Distractions, competing priorities and short-term pressures can easily distract your focus from what matters most. That's why the best leaders create systems and cultures that safeguard their critical priorities.

For example, in my time leading innovation programmes for Olympic teams, the sports that thrived weren't those that chased every shiny new idea. They were the ones that filtered opportunities through their 10%, ensuring every decision aligned with their core priorities. One team leader put it simply: *'If it doesn't strengthen our foundation, it's a distraction.'* That discipline allowed them to focus their energy where it counted, achieving sustained success while others burned out in pursuit of too many goals.

> 'If it doesn't strengthen our foundation, it's a distraction.'

The power of alignment

When everyone in a system understands and commits to the 10%, the impact multiplies. Teams become more than the sum of their parts. Alignment creates cohesion, and cohesion creates momentum. It's the difference between a scattered group of individuals and a unified force working toward a common goal.

Think of an orchestra. Each musician has their part to play, but the conductor ensures that every note aligns to create something greater than any single instrument could achieve alone. Similarly, when teams align their efforts around the 10%, they don't just perform — they excel and thrive.

Find your 10%

So, how do you find your 10%? Start by asking yourself these questions:

What activities or priorities have the greatest impact on our success?

If we stopped doing everything except three things, what would they be?

How can we align our team and resources around these critical priorities?

Once you've identified your 10%, protect it fiercely. Build systems that support focus. Say no to distractions. Trust in the compounding power of clarity and alignment.

The answers to these questions will shape your path to championship-level performance and beyond.

PART TWO SUMMARY

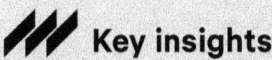 **Key insights**

Your foundation matters — High performance is built on the four interconnected elements of experience, essence, excellence and empowerment. Your past experiences shape who you are, your essence anchors you, excellence is a daily pursuit and empowerment shifts the focus from individual success to collective impact.

Master the Black Arrow — Doubt and hesitation (the 'Black Arrow') are natural, but top performers don't let them dominate. Instead, they master the second thought, shifting from self-doubt to action.

The three lights of leadership — Effective leaders use three perspectives.

- *Floodlight — Seeing the bigger picture and long-term trends.*
- *Spotlight — Focusing on what matters most in the moment.*
- *Greenlight — Knowing when to take decisive action.*

Purpose is the engine — Sustained performance isn't just about skill or talent; it's about having a clear purpose that fuels motivation, alignment and resilience.

Fit-ness is more important than fitness — High-performing teams prioritise how individuals fit together, adapt and work as a cohesive unit over raw talent.

Mastery beyond expertise — Masters don't just accumulate knowledge; they refine their craft, reduce blind spots and constantly evolve.

Mana and presence — True leadership extends beyond words or actions; it's about the energy you bring and the trust you cultivate.

The 10% Principle — The most impactful results come from identifying and focusing on the 10% of activities that truly matter, rather than spreading energy too thin.

/// Common blind spots

Overlooking reflection — Many people go through experiences but fail to extract their lessons, reducing their growth potential.

Chasing perfection instead of excellence — High performers don't seek flawless execution; they focus on continuous improvement.

Ignoring the power of team dynamics — Talent alone doesn't guarantee success; fit-ness and alignment determine sustained performance.

Letting doubt dictate actions — The first thought (Black Arrow) may be fear or hesitation, but the best performers train themselves to replace it with a productive second thought.

Confusing activity with impact — Without identifying the crucial 10% that truly drives success, efforts become scattered and ineffective.

⚑ Amplifying questions

1. *Which past experiences have shaped your performance today, and what lessons are you carrying forward?*
2. *How well do you balance the floodlight (big picture), spotlight (focus) and greenlight (action) in your leadership approach?*
3. *What is the 10% that truly matters in your pursuit of excellence, and how can you protect it from distractions?*

PART THREE

UNLOCKING HIGH PERFORMANCE

AMPLIFY

High performance isn't solely *what you do* — it's *who you are*. No single role carries a team. Success emerges when these roles blend dynamically. In this part, we frame the four core dimensions of leader, learner, contributor and performer.

CHAPTER 15

LEADERS, LEARNERS, PERFORMERS AND CONTRIBUTORS

Be all four

Sustained high performance success, on the water, in the boardroom or on the field, lies in mastering a balance of interconnected mindsets: leader, learner, contributor and performer. These are not titles or fixed roles; they're dynamic behaviours that adapt to the moment and guide how we show up and thrive together.

Working with so many international Olympic coaches and leaders has shown me that true excellence comes from knowing how to dance fluidly between these roles. Think of a sailing crew. The *leader* is the captain, setting the course and ensuring the crew aligns toward the goal. The *learner* is the navigator, scanning the horizon, reading conditions and adapting to changing winds. The *contributor* is the crew, hoisting sails, securing lines and turning plans into motion. And when the storm hits, the *performer*, the helmsman, takes the wheel, steering with focus and precision.

> **No single role carries the team.**

No single role carries the team. It's the ability to shift seamlessly between them that creates collective brilliance. The captain needs the navigator's insights to adjust the course. The navigator depends on the crew's actions to execute decisions. And when pressure peaks, everyone looks to the helmsman to stay calm and steer them through. This interplay — the ability to adapt to circumstances, whether broad (the floodlight), narrow (the spotlight) or decisive (the greenlight) — is what transforms individual strengths into team success.

Mind the gaps

You may recognise people or organisations who are one or two of these roles but not balanced across all four.

Consider a sport obsessed with performance but lacking energy for reviews (learning), team cohesion (collaboration) or vision (leadership). Or a business so focused on strategy and reviews that it struggles to take decisive action.

PART THREE: UNLOCKING HIGH PERFORMANCE

In contrast, the most resilient high performing systems move fluidly between these dimensions. They are not locked into one frame but adapt based on the demands of the moment.

Ask yourself:

- *Which role do I naturally gravitate towards?*
- *Am I the visionary leader, the curious learner, the action-driven contributor or the focused performer?*
- *Which roles challenge me?*

High performers don't just find comfort in their strengths, they develop all four dimensions to become what the moment requires.

Sustained high performers are the individuals and teams that excel over time and are skilled at balancing and blending these roles. They are adaptable captains, curious navigators, diligent crew members and composed helmsmen. They recognise the bigger picture, zoom in on what matters most and act decisively when the time comes. This dynamic rhythm is both mindset and learned skill that fosters enduring success.

High performers are capable of being the captain, the navigator, the crew and the helmsman all rolled into one. A masterful blend of leadership, curiosity, collaboration and execution. Together, these roles form a framework for transformation, propelling teams, organisations and individuals toward their true potential at work and at home.

CHAPTER 16

LEADERS

The best performance leaders I've worked with across multiple Olympic cycles don't seek control or dominance. Leadership is behaviours, not titles. They create environments where people step into their best selves, take responsibility and perform with clarity. Leadership doesn't mean having all the answers — it's about building confidence, capability and alignment in others.

> **Leadership is behaviours, not titles.**

One leader I worked with constantly asked, *'What do you think? How would you solve this?'* instead of jumping in with solutions. They weren't delegating for the sake of it — they were developing problem-solvers. When people learn to navigate challenges independently, the team moves faster, adapts under pressure and sustains success long after the leader has stepped away.

A thriving team is more than just a collection of talented individuals. It's a cohesive network of empowered people who know their strengths and how to use them. Leadership then becomes less about control and more about connection —

building a group that can perform, adapt and succeed without constant supervision.

As a leader, you model the behaviour you want from your team in every area.

Performance conversations

To a performance leader, every conversation is a performance conversation, whether it's a quick check-in or a challenging discussion. How you communicate sets the tone for how issues are resolved, how conflicts are handled and how alignment is achieved.

> **Every conversation is a performance conversation.**

One leader leaned into conflict in a way that stood out. Instead of shutting down a heated disagreement, they asked, 'What's at the root of this tension?' That one question shifted the dynamic. The conversation moved from blame to understanding, creating clarity and strengthening trust. They had a reputation for facing what is hard and uncovering the opportunity within. Their team grew less afraid of conflict as they had repeatedly seen role modelling of opportunity over opposition.

Effective performance conversations require curiosity and intent. Far from finding quick fixes, they're opportunity-seeking to uncover potential and deepen relationships. Leaders who master this don't just address issues; they align their teams and build resilience through every interaction. They uncover opportunities within their team and their system.

Self-awareness, honesty and empathy

Self-awareness is the anchor point before every performance conversation. Leaders who are honest about their strengths and vulnerabilities set the tone for their teams to do the same. They aren't perfect, they're real. They enter every conversation grounded and calm.

During a critical project, one leader paused a meeting and said, *'I think I've been pushing too hard, and it's affecting our focus.'* The room shifted. Far from losing respect, the team rallied around the leader, bringing renewed energy and commitment. That honesty was a trigger that deepened trust and reinforced the team's alignment.

Empathy plays a crucial role, too. High-performance environments can be intense and tense. Leaders who take time to understand their team members' perspectives role model cultures of trust and collaboration. Empathy doesn't mean you agree with everything — it means you hear and see everything, listening and guiding people forward with understanding.

> **No Olympic cycle goes exactly as planned.**

Pressure, uncertainty and loss

No Olympic cycle goes exactly as planned. Pressure is constant. Uncertainty is inevitable. Loss is unavoidable. The leaders who sustain success don't just cope with these — they anticipate them and prepare their teams to respond.

The best athletes and teams I've worked with don't see pressure as a threat. They see it as proof they belong. One Olympic gold medallist put it simply before every final: *'This is not pressure. This is confirmation I'm where I should be.'* That shift in perspective keeps focus sharp when stakes are high.

Uncertainty is another unavoidable challenge. A world-class sailing team I worked with had a simple principle: *'When the wind shifts, so do we.'* The teams and organisations that thrive aren't the ones who expect stability; they are the ones who move fastest when change happens.

Loss is where leadership shows up the most. Across every Olympic cycle, I've seen two responses to loss — those who let it define them and those who let it refine them. The best leaders don't waste time assigning blame or drowning in frustration. They extract lessons, adjust and move forward with sharper clarity. Loss isn't a failure, it's a process of becoming the kind of person or team that wins over time.

> **Loss isn't a failure.**

Empowering culture, performance environments and systems

The best leaders I've worked with across multiple Olympic cycles and high-performance environments don't rely on motivation or control to drive success. Instead, they build cultures and systems that create clarity, ownership and sustained excellence.

In the most effective teams, performance is enabled not forced. These leaders focus on creating environments where expectations are clear, autonomy is supported and people can make the right decisions under pressure. One Olympic coach told me, *'If I have to micromanage, the system is broken'*. The teams that thrive are the ones where leaders design for trust rather than control, ensuring the structure allows people to step up rather than wait for direction.

Empowered environments don't require constant oversight as they create clarity, trust and autonomy, ensuring people take responsibility rather than waiting for instructions. Leaders who understand this design cultures that sustain high performance long after they've moved on.

Five key practices for leaders

1. **Empower, don't control** — Great leaders create environments where people take ownership, step up and grow. They don't solve every problem — they build problem-solvers.

2. **Make every conversation a performance conversation** — Leadership is shaped in daily interactions. The best leaders use dialogue to create clarity, alignment and trust.

3. **Stay self-aware and honest** — Leaders who are real about their strengths and limits set the tone for openness and accountability in their teams.

4. **Lead through pressure, uncertainty and loss** — The best leaders prepare for challenges before they arrive, reframing setbacks as opportunities to refine and improve.

5. **Build systems that sustain success** — Leadership isn't about being involved in every decision. It's about creating an environment where high performance happens without constant intervention.

AMPLIFY

Ask yourself:

- *Am I empowering others to step up or creating quiet dependence?*
- *Do my conversations bring clarity and confidence or confusion and hesitation?*
- *Would my team thrive without me, or am I the bottleneck?*

Next, we'll examine the *learner* role, diving deeper into curiosity, adaptation and continuous improvement.

CHAPTER 17

LEARNERS

Every great performer, leader and team I've worked with across Olympic cycles shares a key trait: they never stop asking questions. Curiosity is what drives discovery, innovation and continuous improvement. It's less about proving what we already know, and more about uncovering what we don't.

Curiosity done well builds trust, strengthens teams and ensures progress never stalls. High performers who stay open to learning create cultures where insights, not egos, drive improvement.

Focus on potential

I worked with a coach who was preparing a cycling team for a world championship. At the end of every training session, she would ask her athletes, *'What's the one thing you noticed today that could help us improve tomorrow?'*

That simple, deliberate question shifted the focus from judging performance to exploring potential. It built a culture where every team member felt empowered to share observations, no matter how small, knowing those insights would shape the next step forward.

Curiosity isn't just a skill for athletes or teams; it's a tool for leadership and self-improvement. When we approach situations with genuine inquiry, we step away from assumptions and open the door to new ideas. It's not about proving what we know but exploring what we can learn.

Curiosity also creates trust. A curious mindset signals to others that their perspectives matter and their contributions are valued. This sense of inclusion fuels engagement, creativity and deeper connections within teams. It reminds us that the best solutions often arise from collective exploration.

Blind spots and problem literacy

In high performance, blind spots — those assumptions we don't see — can quietly sabotage progress. Often, the most urgent issue isn't what we think it is, and effective learners develop *problem literacy*, which is the ability to identify what truly needs solving.

One director of performance believed that the team's bottleneck was physical endurance. However, after digging deeper into feedback and performance data, we found the real issue was pre-race anxiety, which drained the athletes' energy before the start. The team's outcomes dramatically improved when we addressed this hidden barrier with mental readiness training.

Problem literacy begins with questioning the status quo. We ask, *'Are we solving the right problem?'* rather than rushing to implement solutions. This approach creates a disciplined, focused process that directs energy and resources where they'll have the most impact.

When teams commit to uncovering blind spots, they create a culture of honesty and precision. Regularly reflecting on assumptions and welcoming diverse perspectives strengthen their decision-making and execution. Far from avoiding mistakes, they learn to recognise them early and address the true challenge.

Learn from loss

Loss and failure are inevitable in high performance, but they can also be the greatest teachers. The best learners reflect on setbacks and use them as a foundation to move forward stronger.

I worked with a swimmer who narrowly missed Olympic qualification. In the days after, her devastation was palpable, but we reframed the experience. Instead of focusing on what didn't happen, we identified what she gained: personal bests, mental resilience and an opportunity to close key performance gaps. A year later, she returned to qualify and step onto the podium.

> **Loss is a signpost, not a destination.**

Learning from loss requires actively seeking out lessons instead of passively waiting for them to surface. By reflecting on what worked, what didn't and why, we transform setbacks into a roadmap for growth. Loss is simply a signpost, not a destination.

Moving forward from loss also requires perspective. While reflection is essential, facing forwards and focusing on what comes next are equally important. The ability to separate the emotions of failure from the lessons it offers allows learners to grow and thrive.

Polish your craft

Learning doesn't end with knowledge; it requires deliberate practice to translate understanding into mastery. Polishing your craft means focusing on incremental improvements that compound over time.

One rowing coach had a mantra: *'Every stroke counts'*. During training for a regatta, his team focused solely on perfecting the first 10 strokes of every race. This singular focus seemed small but had an outsized impact. By the season's end, the team had mastered their starts, shaving valuable seconds off their times.

> **Mastery is the discipline to show up again and again.**

Polishing the craft also requires resilience. Progress is rarely linear, and setbacks can feel discouraging. High performers understand that even small improvements, made consistently, lead to significant breakthroughs over time. Mastery is the discipline to show up again and again.

This process also builds confidence. Each small improvement reinforces the belief that progress is possible, creating momentum that carries forward. Polishing the craft is a reminder that greatness is built not in dramatic leaps but in consistent, intentional steps.

Adapt and innovate

The final test of a learner's mindset is the ability to respond when the ground shifts. In high performance, conditions change, strategies become obsolete and setbacks arise.

PART THREE: UNLOCKING HIGH PERFORMANCE

I've seen first-hand how the systemic ability to innovate — not just in technology but in thinking — can be the difference between staying competitive and falling behind.

Across multiple Olympic cycles, I worked on performance innovation with Olympic teams from Great Britain and New Zealand. While the two environments were different, one thing stood out. The teams that embraced innovation as a key in their learning mindset were the ones that sustained success. And context is key.

For Team GB, innovation wasn't about chasing the latest technology. It was about refining small details that added up to a competitive edge — where the idea of 'marginal gains' was born. In one Olympic cycle, we focused on race-day environments — how riders recovered between events, how aerodynamics could be fine-tuned and how decision-making under pressure could be trained. The teams that committed to this process — athletes, coaches and support staff — all sharpened their ability to learn and adapt, putting themselves ahead.

> **We built a mindset where challenges were expected, not feared.**

In New Zealand, innovation took a different shape. With fewer resources, the focus was on adaptive problem-solving rather than high-tech advancements. There was no waiting for the 'perfect' solution. Instead, we built a mindset where challenges were expected, not feared. One coach, faced with a major rule change, gathered his team and said, *'Well, that plan's gone — so what can we build instead?'* That shift from frustration to problem-solving became a hallmark of their success.

Innovation in high performance is about having the leadership capacity to stay open, experiment quickly and adapt faster than the competition. Whether in Great Britain's focus on refinement or New Zealand's agility in uncertainty, the teams that led in performance leadership saw innovation not as a department, but as a way of thinking — and that's what made the difference when it mattered most.

Five key practices for learners

1. **Ask better questions** — Learning starts with curiosity. The best performers don't just seek answers; they ask the right questions that unlock growth.
2. **Challenge assumptions** — Effective learners don't accept problems at face value. They step back and ask, 'Are we solving the real issue?'
3. **Turn losses into lessons** — Every setback holds insight. Instead of dwelling on failure, high performers extract the lessons and use them to improve.
4. **Refine through deliberate practice** — Progress comes from consistent, focused effort. Mastery isn't about big leaps but small improvements over time.
5. **Adapt faster than the competition** — Conditions change, and strategies become outdated. The best learners stay agile, ready to innovate when challenges arise.

Ask yourself:

- *Am I asking questions that unlock learning, or just looking for answers?*
- *What assumptions might be limiting my ability to see the real problem?*
- *How well do I turn setbacks into lessons and lessons into action?*

Learning is vital, but without action, insights remain idle. Next, we'll see how the *performer* translates knowledge into execution under pressure.

CHAPTER 18

PERFORMERS

At the heart of sustained high performance is the performer — the one who delivers. They turn ideas into reality, cut through uncertainty and act when the moment demands it.

Performers go beyond executing tasks to shaping outcomes. Instead of waiting for ideal conditions, they make progress in real time. They hold the standard when pressure rises, focus the team when stakes are high, and move the system forward when others hesitate.

Without performers, the best strategies remain concepts and potential never turns into impact.

Control what you can

During one Olympic cycle, I worked with a leader facing a crisis that could have derailed their entire programme. While others were overwhelmed by the magnitude of the problem, the leader asked one simple question: *'What can we control right now?'* That moment shifted the team's focus, cutting through the noise and enabling deliberate, focused action. The team moved forward, step by step, into a performance frame and the crisis passed.

Performers are all about presence. They trust their preparation and instincts, knowing they won't have all the answers but can adapt and deliver. As the explorer Sir Ernest Shackleton famously said, 'Difficulties are just things to overcome, after all'. Performers see challenges as opportunities, grounding their teams in reliability and calm. Their ability to act builds trust, and trust becomes the backbone of high-performance systems.

Turn knowledge into action

Performers focus on action. Knowing what to do is one thing; doing it is another. Performers bridge this gap, turning understanding into outcomes. In high-pressure environments, action often speaks louder than expertise. Progress rarely comes from endless planning, it comes from execution.

> **Performers turn understanding into outcomes.**

A world championship team I worked with had everything — cutting-edge data, strategic plans and technical expertise, yet they were paralysed. Training sessions were full of debates over details. Team meetings became exercises in over-analysis. Every decision felt like it needed one more round of validation. Progress stalled.

Finally, a senior leader stood up and said, *'Enough. What's the one thing we can execute today?'* That moment was a turning point. The focus moved from endless refinement to deliberate execution. They started making adjustments, testing approaches and learning in real time rather than in theory.

Performers simplify complexity. They don't let the fear of imperfection delay progress. They identify the next critical action, execute it and refine as they go. They understand that winning isn't about having every answer in advance — it's about the ability to make the right move at the right time.

Master fear and conflict

Fear is part of the performer's landscape. Instead of avoiding it, performers harness it as energy. Whether it's the butterflies of anticipation or the tension of conflict, they channel these forces into purposeful action.

Before an Olympic semi-final, one athlete I knew described their nerves as a storm in their stomach — a tightening, an uncontrollable rush of energy. They tried to fight it, to force themselves into a state of calm, but the more they resisted, the worse it got.

Their coach pulled them aside and said, *'That's not fear — it's fuel; it is your advantage'.* Instead of trying to eliminate fear, they channelled it. When the moment arrived, they stepped into it with a new perspective — using that nervous energy to sharpen their focus rather than weaken their performance.

Rather than avoiding fear, performers train for it, work with it and use it to sharpen their edge. The same applies to conflict. One Olympic leader put it perfectly: *'When people argue, it's never just about the disagreement — it's about what they care about'.* Performers lean into tough conversations, not to dominate, but to uncover what really matters and align the team.

Those who perform when the emotions are high and the conflict is high help steady the environment for everyone around them. Their ability to stay composed, focus on what matters and engage in difficult conversations with clarity makes them a stabilising force in high-stakes moments.

Deliver under pressure

In critical moments, focus and communication are non-negotiable. Performers thrive because they align themselves and others around what matters most, clearly cutting through distractions.

In a decisive world cup match in basketball, I noticed how the two teams responded to pressure in very different ways. One coach pulled their players in and said just two things: *'Tight defence. Play the edges'.* That was it — two clear instructions. The players locked in, aligned and executed.

On the other side, the opposing coach was firing out commands every few seconds — shouting names, calling plays and reacting to every movement. The players looked overwhelmed, uncertain and scattered. The team collapsed under the weight of too much noise.

> **Clarity is a competitive advantage.**

Performers understand that clarity is a competitive advantage. They cut through the distractions and deliver the right message at the right moment. They also master the second thought — their first instinct might be reactive, emotional or scattered, but they train themselves to pause, refocus and act with precision.

In the end, performers succeed because they bring calm to chaos. Their focus becomes an anchor, and their communication ensures alignment, encouraging people and systems forward when it matters most.

Five key practices for performers

1. **Focus on what you can control** — Performers cut through uncertainty, act with composure and keep teams anchored in high-pressure situations.
2. **Turn knowledge into action** — They don't wait for perfect conditions. They simplify decisions, take action and adjust as they go.
3. **Use fear and conflict productively** — Instead of avoiding fear or tension, they channel it into focus and use conflict to align teams.
4. **Stay clear under pressure** — They communicate simply and decisively, keeping teams focused on what matters most.
5. **Provide stability** — By staying composed, they help others perform, creating a calm and focused environment.

Ask yourself:

- *Am I focusing on what I can control, or am I getting distracted by what I can't?*
- *Am I turning knowledge into action, or am I stuck in overthinking and hesitation?*
- *When pressure rises, do I bring clarity and composure, or do I add to the noise?*

CHAPTER 19

CONTRIBUTORS

In high performance, vision without execution is just theory. The best strategies, ideas and leadership mean little without people who bring them to life.

Contributors do exactly that. They are the engine room of progress, turning ideas into results, keeping momentum alive and ensuring that high-performance teams don't just prepare well but deliver consistently.

While leaders set direction, learners discover new ways forward and performers rise under pressure, it's contributors who drive the daily execution, ensuring that potential translates into impact. Without them, even the best-laid plans remain as words on paper.

Turn intentions into impact

I once worked with a leader who put it simply. *'You can have the clearest strategy in the world, but without someone to carry it out, it's just a map with no journey.'*

Contributors make sure the journey happens. They ask, *'What needs to happen next?'* and focus their energy on meaningful action — turning chaos into clarity and ensuring the team is always moving towards shared goals.

In one Olympic cycle, I saw this in action with a contributor on an elite cycling team. They weren't the lead coach, the sports scientist or the technical director. Their official role was in physiotherapy, yet their impact stretched far beyond that. They became the glue of the operation, ensuring that training schedules aligned with nutrition, that mechanics and riders communicated seamlessly and that the smallest performance details were addressed before they became problems. They weren't in the spotlight, but their ability to keep every moving part synchronised was the difference between an average campaign and a medal-winning performance.

High-performance teams are often defined by those contributors who make the complex feel seamless.

Action over motion

Not all movement creates progress. Some of the busiest teams I've worked with were the least effective — not for lack of effort, but for lack of clarity. Activity alone is not a measure of success. The best contributors don't just stay busy; they know the difference between momentum and movement. They focus relentlessly on what shifts the dial.

In one Olympic programme, I worked with a national team that had world-class talent, top-tier funding and access to cutting-edge technology. Yet, despite their resources, they were stagnating.

PART THREE: UNLOCKING HIGH PERFORMANCE

The training calendar was packed, the support team was working around the clock and athletes were logging exhausting hours — but results weren't improving.

When we stepped back and examined what was actually moving performance forward, we realised much of the training was focused on volume rather than effectiveness. The team was caught in a cycle of doing more rather than doing better.

Once they streamlined their approach — prioritising high-intensity training blocks over excessive volume, refining their recovery strategies and cutting out the 'filler' sessions — performance surged. The lesson was clear: effort without focus is just fatigue.

> **Activity alone is not a measure of success.**

I saw a similar pattern while working with a global business leader in the middle of a major restructuring. Their executive team was constantly in strategy meetings, refining plans, analysing risks and debating scenarios. Meanwhile, their competitors were making moves.

The turning point came when the CEO, frustrated by the endless loops of discussion, walked into a meeting and said: *'Decisions, not discussions. What three actions will we take by the end of this meeting?'* The dynamic changed instantly. Instead of circling around ideas, they began committing to action. Within weeks, they moved from paralysis to execution, gaining back ground they had lost.

The best contributors don't mistake motion for progress. They cut through the noise, simplify the complex and ensure that every action contributes to the bigger picture. It's not about doing more — it's about doing what matters.

Build habits and systems

We know sustained high performance is built on systems, not bursts of motivation or one-off moments of brilliance. The most consistent performers in elite sport or high-stakes business don't rely on inspiration to drive progress. They create structures that remove friction, making success inevitable.

One Olympic leader had a simple philosophy: *'The medal isn't won on the day — it's earned in the thousands of small decisions made long before.'* They weren't talking about talent, luck or effort. They were talking about *systems* — the accumulation of routines, processes and habits that allow athletes to step onto the podium with confidence, knowing their preparation has already delivered the outcome. Confidence comes from preparation.

> **Confidence comes from preparation.**

I've seen this play out in environments where success was designed, not just hoped for. One Olympic cycling programme built a training structure where nothing was left to chance. Recovery schedules were mapped with military precision. Equipment was optimised to eliminate marginal inefficiencies. Team operations were fine-tuned so athletes didn't waste energy on logistics, admin or second-guessing decisions. By the time competition arrived, winning was the natural result of a system that left no room for failure.

Contrast that with teams or businesses that rely on last-minute surges, overhauls or 'stepping up when it counts'. They burn out, miss details and scramble when the pressure hits. They hope for success rather than build for it.

> **Systems are the votes cast long before the result is announced.**

As James Clear puts it, *'Every action you take is a vote for the person you wish to become.'* Systems are the votes cast long before the result is announced. The best contributors understand that consistency is a competitive advantage. They don't wait for conditions to be perfect — they build structures that make excellence the default.

Contribution through collective momentum

High performers don't operate in isolation. The best contributors make sure the team moves forward.

Collaboration is more than working together — it's making every action count. I've seen Olympic teams stacked with talent fall short because, despite individual brilliance, they weren't aligned. And I've seen teams with less talent outperform expectations because everyone understood their role in making the whole system work.

One Olympic cycling team I worked with had a rider who wasn't the strongest or fastest, but their impact was undeniable. They knew exactly when to push the pace, when to support a teammate and when to hold back.

The best contributors create momentum and rhythm. The steady, reliable force that transforms potential into collective reality. Their work may not always take the spotlight, but the entire system falters without them. Their ability to move the team forward consistently and collaboratively creates a lasting legacy.

Five key practices for contributors

1. **Turn intentions into impact** — Execution is everything. Contributors don't wait for the perfect moment — they identify the next best step and take it.
2. **Focus on progress, not just activity** — Busy doesn't mean effective. The best contributors cut through distractions and prioritise what truly shifts performance.
3. **Build systems** — Success isn't about last-minute intensity; it's about well-designed habits and processes that make excellence inevitable.
4. **Create collective momentum** — High performance is a team game. Contributors align their actions to the bigger mission, ensuring progress is shared.
5. **Simplify and execute** — Complexity can stall action. The best contributors clarify priorities, remove unnecessary steps and get things done.

Ask yourself:

- *Am I turning ideas into action, or am I getting stuck in planning?*
- *Is my effort moving the team forward, or just keeping me busy?*
- *What systems can I build today that will make success easier tomorrow?*

PART THREE SUMMARY

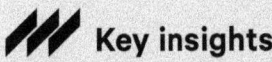 **Key insights**

High performance is fluid, not fixed — Success comes from moving between being a leader, learner, contributor and performer as the situation demands. Sticking to one role limits growth and impact.

Leaders empower, not control — Great leaders create environments where people step up, take ownership and perform without micromanagement. They guide, align and build trust.

Learners unlock growth — Learners fuel progress by asking better questions, challenging assumptions and adapting fast. They see setbacks as learning moments, not failures.

Performers execute under pressure — Performers act when it counts. They cut through uncertainty, focus on what matters and deliver results instead of getting stuck in over-planning.

Contributors drive momentum — Contributors turn strategy into action. They simplify complexity, focus on impact and keep the team moving forward, avoiding pointless busyness.

Mastering fear and conflict is essential — High performers don't avoid pressure or tough conversations — they use them for focus, alignment and resilience. Growth happens when challenges are faced head-on.

Systems beat talent alone — Sustained success is built, not hoped for. Leaders create strong systems, learners refine them, contributors keep them running and performers execute within them.

Common blind spots

Getting stuck in one role — Excelling in one area (e.g., leadership or execution) but neglecting others creates an imbalance. A leader who never learns stops growing. A performer who doesn't contribute weakens the team.

Confusing activity with progress — Contributors can mistake busyness for impact. Effort should drive meaningful results, not just create motion.

Over-planning and under-executing — Some learners and leaders get stuck in strategy and fail to act. Performers bridge this gap by executing and adjusting.

Avoiding pressure and conflict — Leaders and performers who dodge difficult conversations or high-pressure moments miss key opportunities for growth, alignment and resilience.

Over-reliance on individual talent — Without strong systems and teamwork, even the most gifted leaders, learners, contributors or performers will struggle to sustain long-term success.

 Amplifying questions

1. Which role (leader, learner, contributor, performer) do I default to, and where do I need to grow?
2. Am I focusing on what truly moves the needle, or just staying busy?
3. How well does my team balance leadership, learning, contribution and execution? Where are the gaps?

PART FOUR

SUSTAINING HIGH PERFORMANCE

AMPLIFY

We've explored the literacy of high performance — what it takes to truly understand the game. We've dug into the foundations, the roles you play and how they shape success. Now, we shift focus to something just as critical. The environment you create.

High performance doesn't happen in isolation. The best don't just train harder; they operate in environments that make thriving the norm. After thousands of interviews with medallists, non-medallists, repeat winners, coaches and leaders, three things stand out in the best performance environments. Simplicity, alignment and well-being.

Get the environment right, and performance flows. Less friction, more focus. Less clutter, more clarity. People don't just perform — they sustain, adapt and grow.

This section is about making that happen.

CHAPTER 20

THREE PILLARS OF SUSTAINED SUCCESS

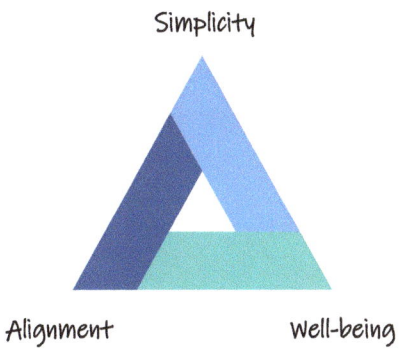

High performance, at its core, is communication and energy. The best teams, businesses and families don't just *work harder* — they work *smarter*. Their environments have less friction, fewer blind spots, more cohesion and deeper unity.

After years of research — thousands of interviews with medallists, non-medallists, repeat champions, coaches and leaders — one truth became clear: some people thrive while others stall, and the difference is not talent or effort. It's the *environment*. When we looked under the hood, we found that the best environments were built on three universal pillars of simplicity, alignment and well-being.

Some teams, businesses and even families have lost sight of these, camouflaging their performance with too much clutter and busy. But in every championship-capable environment, these three pillars were the key drivers — the levers that, when pulled, created real, lasting change.

Simplicity clears the path. It's not about stripping things down to nothing; it's about removing what *doesn't serve*, removing the unnecessary. The best teams, like the best-designed ecosystems, embrace natural complexity without adding unnecessary friction. Confusing processes, outdated structures and layers of noise slow people down. Simplicity removes resistance, sharpens focus and lets performance flow.

Alignment makes everything work in unison. Without it, even the most talented individuals work against each other — like a rowing team paddling out of sync. When roles, goals and values are aligned, momentum builds, energy compounds and progress flows.

Well-being fuels it all. A high-performance environment without well-being is like a high-performance engine without oil. It might run fast, but it won't run for long. Well-being is more than personal health; it's about creating systemic conditions where people operate at their best *consistently*. It's the foundation of resilience, adaptability and sustained energy under pressure.

PART FOUR: SUSTAINING HIGH PERFORMANCE

These three key pillars are not silos. They are deeply interconnected. Simplicity removes clutter, making alignment easier. Alignment reduces friction, fueling well-being. Well-being sustains energy, which allows simplicity to take hold.

When you get the roles right and understand the levers to pull, you create environments that don't just perform — they sustain, adapt and grow.

This is true in sport. In business. In families. In life.

When we strip away the distractions, this is what remains. These are the forces that drive *real* systemic change. The next chapters break down how to build these pillars into the environments you lead. That means success isn't a one-off, it's something that lasts.

CHAPTER 21

WELL-BEING BRINGS ENERGY

Well-being goes beyond simply offering fitness programmes or boosting morale. It is creating the systemic energy needed to achieve long-term success for teams and organisations.

Unlike personal wellness (such as maintaining exercise routines or healthy habits) or general well-being (like feeling satisfied with a life well lived), I use the term *performance well-being*. It is well-being with a wider and more collective purpose and focuses on the shared energy within a group that drives its success and resilience.

It looks like this.

```
            Performance
            well-being
                △
               ╱ ╲
              ╱   ╲
             ╱     ╲
            ╱       ╲
           ╱         ╲
          ╱_____╲
       Wellness      Well-being
```

Performance well-being is the systemic energy that fuels, connects and sustains high performance across the entire organisation. It ensures that people and teams don't just function — they thrive.

Wellness is the foundation of individual vitality — physical health, recovery and daily habits that support sustained energy and resilience.

Well-being is the emotional and psychological balance that shapes fulfilment, motivation and long-term engagement in work and life.

The impact of well-being

Organisations that embed systemic well-being into their culture enhance workplace morale and create measurable performance gains. Aon's *2022-2023 Global Well-being Survey* found that prioritising well-being can improve company performance by 11% to 55%, demonstrating that organisations investing in employee health and energy unlock a competitive advantage.[14]

> **Well-being and productivity are interdependent forces.**

This impact extends beyond the organisation itself. McKinsey Health Institute's research highlighted that investing in employee health could increase global GDP by 4% to 12%, emphasising that well-being is both an individual benefit and an economic driver.[15] High-performing organisations recognise that well-being and productivity are not separate initiatives but interdependent forces.

The most effective performance well-being strategies go beyond surface-level perks like free gym memberships and healthy lunches. Instead, they cultivate an environment where energy flows freely, enabling individuals and teams to operate at their best. By integrating physical, mental and social well-being into their operational framework, organisations create the conditions for sustained high performance.

Teams with strong performance well-being are cohesive and resilient under pressure. They create a space where innovation thrives, as the energy flow supports collaboration and idea-sharing. Conversely, when even one point of the well-being triangle falters, the system becomes sluggish, with teams losing focus and momentum. This underscores the importance of monitoring the energy-health of all aspects of the system, as a breakdown in one area can create a ripple effect that impacts overall performance.

Look for growth

In addition to maintaining balance within the triangle, leaders can use this framework to identify areas for growth. Performance well-being requires a systems-wide view, with performance leaders evaluating workflows, team dynamics and processes to get a read on the energy-health of their system.

By viewing performance well-being as a foundational part of organisational success, leaders can fundamentally change how they design and support their teams. Instead of merely aiming to improve individual productivity, they take a broader perspective and ask critical questions such as: How does energy flow across our team and organisation? Are we fostering an environment where energy is replenished, especially after demanding deadlines and high-stakes projects and commitments? Do team members feel a clear connection between their personal well-being and the overarching goals of the organisation?

Keep departments aligned

Performance leadership also is astutely aware of how alignment across working groups, departments and individual roles supports performance well-being. When communication and purpose are misaligned, teams often lose sight of how their work contributes to the bigger picture. There is an energy drain in this misalignment. Leaders can re-establish clarity by providing regular feedback and revisiting goals to ensure they remain relevant and achievable. Providing spaces where teams can reflect and recharge — whether through intentional pauses between major projects, team-building activities or moments of celebration — fosters a more balanced and sustainable workflow.

Energised systems vs. isolated energy

People and performance thrive in energised systems, where the team's collective energy elevates individual efforts. These systems are characterised by shared goals, trust and open communication, creating an environment where collaboration flourishes.

When Satya Nadella became the CEO of Microsoft, he transformed the organisation's competitive culture into one that prioritised empathy, collaboration and trust. This cultural shift revitalised Microsoft, enhancing both morale and performance.

In contrast, systems plagued by energy friction, such as unclear communication, lack of direction or internal power struggles, drain even the most dedicated individuals.

In one organisation I observed where onboarding was rushed and retirements were ignored, these missed opportunities sent the message that people were undervalued, leading to decreased morale and trust. Energy friction doesn't just affect individuals; it ripples outward, creating inefficiencies and disengagement across the team.

Energised systems approach every event — onboarding a new hire or honouring a retiree — as an opportunity to reinforce purpose, connection and systemic energy-health.

These systems encourage ongoing dialogue and collaboration. Regular team check-ins, shared decision-making and a culture of appreciation keep energy flowing positively. When every team member feels they have a voice and that their work aligns with the organisation's purpose, the result is a stronger, more resilient system.

Energised systems provide mechanisms to anticipate and address potential energy drains. For instance, a company might establish feedback loops where employees can flag inefficiencies or suggest improvements.

> **By actively addressing points of energy friction, organisations prevent burnout and promote innovation and engagement.**

By actively addressing points of energy friction, organisations prevent burnout and promote innovation and engagement.

In practice, leaders play a crucial role in creating and maintaining energised systems. They set the tone by modelling empathy, ensuring clarity in communication and valuing the contributions of every team member. The shift from isolated energy at the individual level to energised systems isn't just about fixing what's broken — it's cultivating a culture where energy is seen as a shared and renewable resource.

The energy balance sheet

A helpful tool to help leaders measure and manage energy is using an energy balance sheet, which tracks what gives and takes energy within a system. Think of energy like money:

Energy assets are activities or relationships that boost energy (e.g., meaningful work or supportive teammates).

Energy liabilities drain energy (e.g., unclear expectations or negative behaviours).

I worked with an Olympic support team that, despite excellent time management, arrived at the Games completely exhausted. Their focus on managing time instead of energy led to burnout. As we identified energy drains and shifting priorities, they improved recovery, individual well-being and collective performance.

Steps to using the energy balance sheet

1. List your energy assets and liabilities.
2. Track trends over time (what's getting worse, staying the same or getting better).

3. Adjust priorities (keep, start, stop) to increase assets and reduce liabilities.
4. Repeat.

This approach shifts the focus from doing more to doing what matters most and measuring and making visible the currency of 'collective energy'. The best systems are highly skilled at creating powerful habits. Make energy mapping one of your own powerful habits.

I've worked with many high performing leaders and systems who implement the energy balance sheet. They identified systemic shifts in behaviour, belonging and cohesion within their teams. Those shifts translated into higher performance.

Impacting the balance sheet

Our performance leadership plays a big role in keeping energy flowing. Good leaders help teams stay clear, aligned and resilient by managing energy effectively.

How do leaders lift energy?

They **clarify goals** and show how each person's work fits into the bigger picture.

They **reduce friction** by fixing inefficient processes and unclear communication.

They **build trust** by being empathetic and authentic.

They **invest in culture**, using rituals like team recognition and celebrations to strengthen connections.

These aspects are bread and butter components in many organisations, but they often sit outside the balance sheet. When the key currency of energy is visible in your world, in your language, your habits and measurements there is a fundamental systemic shift in awareness and performance. Energy is distributed.

No one 'owns' energy. When we embed it into the working currency of our teams and organisations, we move from focusing on components to focusing on the collective distributed flow of energy across our system.

Leaders who emphasise energy as a shared resource, empower their teams to drive, thrive and revive.

The energy of skilful coping

A meaningful life comes with stress. A Gallup Poll confirms that those who find deep meaning in their work and lives report higher levels of stress but also higher fulfilment.[16] The difference? It's not about avoiding stress but coping with it well.

This is skilful coping — the ability to navigate high-pressure situations with clarity, control and confidence. It's the difference between stress being a burden and stress becoming a driver of progress. Olympic athletes often view stress as a source of motivation rather than a barrier. One cyclist shared, *'If I'm not stressed, it means the event doesn't matter. The pressure reminds me of what's at stake and pushes me to focus.'*

Years ago, I met the Dreyfus brothers, originators of the novice-to-expert spectrum. After our discussion, they sent me their book on skilful coping. I recognised instantly what I had already seen in high-performance sport. The best athletes, teams and leaders had developed this skill deeply. They weren't avoiding stress. They were using it.

In the best teams and organisations, stress doesn't break people, it binds them. High-performance systems don't eliminate stress; they make coping visible and shiftable. And when coping improves, energy flows, momentum builds and sustained success follows.

Understanding and leveraging stress begins with reframing it. It is a source of energy on the balance sheet. Teams and individuals who view stress as a challenge to overcome, rather than a threat to avoid, develop resilience and maintain focus under pressure. Stress becomes a tool for learning, harnessing energy and driving performance to new levels.

What skilful coping looks like

Reframe stress — Teach teams to see challenges as opportunities. A tight deadline isn't pressure, it's a chance to test creativity and efficiency. A difficult client is an opportunity to sharpen communication and problem-solving skills.

Foster resilience — Equip teams with practical tools, such as team reflections, scenario planning and structured recovery, so they are ready for challenges before they arise.

Lead by example — Leaders who stay calm and clear-headed in tough moments set the tone for their teams. Their response signals that pressure is normal and manageable.

Create recovery periods — After high-stakes work, allow for intentional recovery — time off, debriefs or small celebrations.

High performance isn't about pushing endlessly; it's about knowing when to refuel.

Share the load — Teams with strong coping skills don't leave stress to individuals. They manage it collectively, supporting each other through high-pressure periods.

Teams with strong coping skills thrive in energised systems. They share responsibility for managing stress collectively and support one another through high-pressure periods. In these environments, stress is embraced as a driver of progress.

In energised systems, stress becomes a shared challenge that brings teams closer together. Instead of breaking under pressure, these teams find strength in their collective ability to adapt and grow. Leaders play a critical role in fostering this mindset, ensuring that stress serves as a catalyst for innovation and collaboration rather than a source of division. The big question is whether your system is boosting and balancing energy or draining it.

Ask yourself:

- *How well does energy flow in my team, and what's draining it?*
- *Are we creating a system that keeps people energised, or just fixing burnout when it happens?*
- *Do we see pressure and stress as something to avoid, or as a tool for growth and performance?*

CHAPTER 22

SIMPLICITY BRINGS CLARITY

Simplicity means focusing on what's important and ensuring clarity in every action. I call this strategic simplicity. My first book *Simplify* focuses on keeping the overall performance system simple. In this chapter we drill into the use of simplicity in our performance leadership.

In high-performing teams, strategic simplicity allows everyone to concentrate on their goals and understand exactly how to achieve them. By reducing distractions and conserving energy, simplicity creates opportunities for a deeper focus on meaningful work, leading to better outcomes.

Aiming for harmony

The biggest barrier to high performance isn't a lack of effort, talent or resources — it's clutter. Unnecessary complexity, redundant processes and bloated systems conceal clarity and disrupt harmony. Instead of energy flowing towards meaningful work, it gets trapped in confusion, hesitation and inefficiency.

A high-performing team had everything — talent, experience and ambition — but they were stuck. Progress felt slow, energy was drained and momentum was nowhere to be found. It wasn't because they lacked skill; they were buried under layers of unnecessary steps, constant firefighting and meetings that solved nothing. They were busy, but not moving forward.

When we stripped it back — eliminated noise, cut away what didn't add value and focused only on what mattered — everything shifted. They were the same people with the same goals, but now they had clarity. They could finally see what was important. Friction disappeared and progress started to flow.

This happens everywhere. In business, in sport, in families. We overcomplicate, overthink and overcrowd. Clarity is buried. The more clutter we remove, the more obvious the right path becomes.

The true cost of clutter

Clutter slows decisions. When everything seems important, nothing gets prioritised. Clutter exhausts people. The brain wastes energy navigating unnecessary complexity. Clutter conceals what works — the best ideas, processes and actions get buried under noise.

One sports team that used 10 different apps to track performance. The sheer number of tools overwhelmed the team. Each was designed for a specific task, but none were integrated and the lack of connection made processes inefficient. I worked with the team to replace those 10 apps with a single integrated system. The change saved time and energy and revolutionised how the team operated. By cutting out unnecessary tools and streamlining their workflow, the team found new clarity, focus and a significant improvement in overall performance.

Creating clarity and harmony

The best systems let people do their best work without resistance. Better medals...better results...better flow. The real question isn't *'How much more can we add?'* It's *'How much can we remove to see things clearly?'*

The path to clarity has three steps:

Remove then refine — Instead of adding more solutions, strip away what isn't working.

Simplify decision-making — If a process has too many steps, challenge why they exist.

Make space for flow — When friction is removed, momentum builds naturally.

Complexity isn't the enemy

The best systems in the world are complex, but they work because they are free from unnecessary complications.

Look at nature. The human body, the weather, a rainforest ecosystem — all are complex, interconnected and constantly adapting. Yet they hum along, self-regulating, because everything has a role and nothing is wasted.

Your body doesn't overthink digestion. A forest doesn't add unnecessary steps to its nutrient cycle. The planets don't schedule extra meetings to stay in orbit. They function because they are complex without being complicated.

What happens when a complication is introduced?

A broken bone? The body adapts, laying down new tissue. A missing predator? The ecosystem shifts to rebalance.

The trap of complication

Sometimes, though, the adaptation doesn't work. Instead of solving the issue, it creates more problems.

A weak knee leads to an altered running pattern, which leads to hip pain.

A new policy creates confusion, so another policy is added to clarify it.

A lie needs five more lies to cover it up.

That is how complication creeps in. Not as a deliberate choice, but as a reaction. When something goes wrong, the instinct is to add more rules, tools and steps, rather than stripping away what no longer serves the system.

I call this winner's bloat. Successful teams and organisations add layers over time — new protocols, new processes, new 'essential' tools — until they are weighed down by their own systems.

I worked with an Olympic team that had built layer upon layer of performance tracking, meetings and specialised committees. At first, these helped them stay ahead. But over time, they became barriers instead of boosters. Too many steps. Too much noise. The team wasn't performing worse because they lacked ability — they were drowning in their own complexity.

Once we stripped back the unnecessary, clarity returned, friction disappeared and performance surged.

The best systems — whether in sport, business or nature — aren't simple, but they are uncomplicated. They allow complexity to function without interference.

Complexity needs space to run. Complication chokes it. The challenge isn't to remove complexity, it's to strip away what gets in its way.

Cut clutter and find flow

High performers rely on systems that create flow. When processes are cluttered, overcomplicated and full of unnecessary steps, they disrupt momentum and make performance harder than it needs to be.

Simplicity is about removing friction so that energy moves to what matters. Flow is often seen as a psychological state, but in performance, flow is built through preparation and system design.

A key difference emerged across my research into medallists and non-medallists: flow was not random — it was structured. The athletes and teams that performed under pressure had simplified systems. They had removed unnecessary steps, distractions and inefficiencies, so when the moment came to perform, they weren't thinking about their environment or battling their own system.

In high performance, flow comes from preparation, not chance.

This aligns with the work of Mihaly Csikszentmihalyi, who studied flow and found it occurs when challenge and skill are in balance and external distractions are reduced.[17] In high performance, flow comes from preparation, not chance.

From clutter to clarity

One leader introduced a simplicity audit, where every team member could suggest changes to reduce unnecessary work. The response was overwhelming, as everyone saw the clutter but had never been asked to remove it.

Out of this, they developed a rule: *'One in, one out'.*

For every new system, process or initiative introduced, something had to be removed. This forced clarity. It stopped layering complexity on top of complexity. It made them more deliberate about what they added and helped them see their system as a whole, not isolated parts.

The result? Fewer distractions. More energy where it mattered. A system that worked for them, not against them.

Flow is built, not found

Flow separates those who sustain performance from those who struggle under pressure. Flow is something you prepare for, not something you stumble into. The more you cut clutter and refine your system, the more natural performance becomes.

Before you add something new, ask:

Does this fuel flow or disrupt it?

What would we remove to make space for it?

PART FOUR: SUSTAINING HIGH PERFORMANCE

Are we designing for performance or adding layers without thinking?

High performers don't fight their systems — they move through them. The more you cut the clutter, the easier it is to find flow.

Simplicity audit

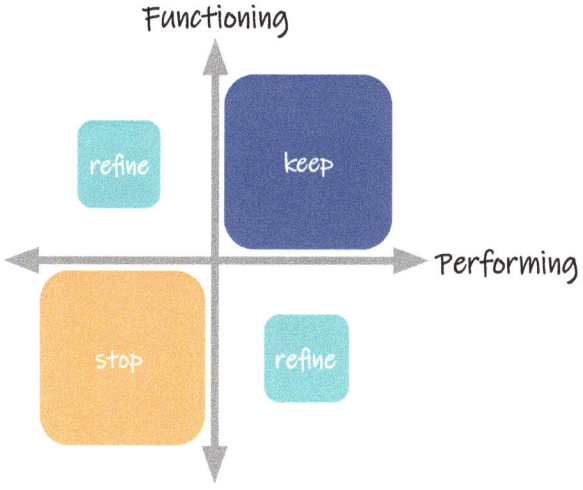

We've talked about the energy balance sheet and how everything in a system either fuels or drains energy. The simplicity audit is how you make visible where that energy is going. It shines a light on what's working, what's slowing you down and what needs to go.

Too many systems are weighed down by legacy practices — things that once had value but now hide clarity instead of fuelling it. These practices stick around because:

- They were introduced to solve a problem that no longer exists.
- They seemed helpful once, but no one has checked if they still add value.
- They were meant as temporary fixes but became permanent habits.

A simplicity audit puts every practice, habit and system through a performance filter. It asks, does this actually help, or is it just something we've always done?

What stays and what goes

Every process, meeting, habit or tool falls into one of four categories:

Keep — High-functioning, high-performing. These are the big rocks, the core practices that work smoothly and drive performance. For example, a daily 10-minute team huddle that removes blockers, sharpens priorities and fuels momentum.

Refine — High-functioning but low-performing. These things run smoothly but aren't clearly driving results. Instead of removing them, they need adjustment to make them work harder. For example, collecting data that never gets used for decisions. It's not broken, but it needs refining so the insight is clear and actionable.

Stop — Low-functioning, low-performing. This is where legacy clutter hides — things that create friction but no longer add real value. For example, regular 'check-in' meetings with no clear purpose. People attend out of habit, but they don't improve performance, and the same conversations happen elsewhere. These drain time and energy. Cut them.

Refine — Low-functioning but high-performing. These practices drive results but are harder than they should be, either due to inefficiencies or unnecessary complications. For example, a high-value performance review system that takes too long to complete. The insight is great, but the process is slow and exhausting. It needs simplifying to maintain impact without wasting energy.

Keep energy flowing where it matters

The best teams, businesses and systems don't run on more — they run on better. They regularly audit what they do, remove what no longer serves them and refine what could work harder.

Before you add another initiative, ask:

Does it fuel clarity or hide it?

Does it function smoothly without extra effort?

Would we notice if we stopped doing it?

Simplicity isn't about doing less — it's about making energy flow to what matters with less resistance. What would happen if you cut everything that isn't earning its place?

Simplicity is a habit

Simplicity isn't something you achieve, it's something you protect. Left unchecked, complexity creeps in. Winning teams and organisations often carry layers of past solutions — things that once worked but no longer fit. Instead of questioning them, many systems default to what has always been done. They get caught when the world shifts and they don't.

The best don't fall into this trap. They keep the big rocks clear and visible to leadership and everyone in the team. They know that if everything is important, nothing is protected.

A hallmark of championship-capable systems is their ability to collectively articulate what matters most and, critically, to protect it. This isn't theoretical. In the research across repeat medallists and non-medallists, we asked a simple but revealing question:

What would you keep, start and stop for the next event?

The answers exposed a fundamental difference. Repeat medallists made up only 5% of the population but owned 80% of the stops. They were far more deliberate about:

- *What they protected* — *the non-negotiables that drove performance.*
- *What they kept simple* — *so focus wasn't lost in unnecessary complexity.*
- *When to say no* — *so time, energy and resources weren't diluted.*

This discipline is no accident. The best don't just ask, 'What else do we need?' They also ask, 'What no longer fits?' They treat simplicity as a habit.

Championship teams protect simplicity

One high-performing team I worked with introduced quarterly simplicity reviews. These involved checking if their systems still served their goals. They asked:

- What's working well?
- What's slowing us down?
- What have we added that isn't pulling its weight?

By questioning their system, they kept it sharp. They didn't wait for inefficiencies to pile up, they caught them early.

Simplicity is something you protect, not just achieve. When it becomes a habit, it shapes culture. People stop accepting clutter as normal. They actively protect clarity. And that's the difference between teams that perform once and teams that perform again and again.

Ask yourself:

- *What's adding unnecessary complexity to my work, and how can I simplify it?*
- *Do my team's tools and processes help us focus, or are they slowing us down?*
- *How can I communicate more clearly so that everyone knows what truly matters?*

CHAPTER 23

ALIGNMENT BRINGS COHESION

High performance isn't a solo act.

Even in sports where an athlete takes the stage alone, their success is built on a foundation of alignment, with coaches, support staff, teammates and systems all pulling in the same direction.

At its core, high performance is about communication, and alignment ensures that every role in the system is clear, connected and synchronised with their words and actions. When roles are well-defined, teams move with cohesion, purpose and unity. Much like rowers in a boat are synchronised in their effort, as each pulls their weight toward a shared goal. Without alignment, energy is wasted, confusion sets in and performance suffers.

The leadership rudder

Alignment starts with clarity of purpose, values and principles that steer the collective energy of individuals toward a shared goal.

Without it, even the best-intentioned teams can find themselves working at odds, overlapping or pulling in different directions. High performance is about working in sync, not working harder.

> **High performance is about working in sync, not working harder.**

I start every project by helping individuals and teams uncover and even revisit their core values, principles and purpose. You would be surprised how many teams and organisations assume these are well understood, especially when they have plastered the key words across the walls in big letters.

Yet most people are unaware. This is evident in the many reviews and interviews I have conducted comparing medallist and non-medallist systems. The best performing systems had values, purpose and principles that were clearly and consistently articulated and described across the system. The consistency stood out in language and behaviours. It is an alignment game changer.

The power of a clear rudder

Alignment is like the rudder of a ship. Whether it's a giant cargo ship, a cruise liner or a high-speed racing yacht, the rudder is small compared to the vessel itself. But its impact is enormous. Without a rudder, the ship drifts aimlessly, no matter how powerful the engines. The engines (individuals in the team) provide the drive, but the rudder (the team's purpose, values and principles) determines where the energy is directed. When alignment is strong, every person becomes their own engine, pushing in the same direction, guided by the same set of core principles.

When the rudder is unclear, misalignment takes over. This isn't intentionally bad choices; it's about committed individuals lacking the necessary clarity to make the right ones.

The difference between a medal-winning team and one that falls short most often reveals areas of misalignment. In my research, one of the clearest distinctions was that the best teams don't leave alignment to chance. Their decision-making isn't reinvented in every moment of pressure. Their values, purpose and principles act as guides, making tough decisions easier and ensuring that every role has a clear lane to operate in.

Take the All Blacks rugby team. They have individuals with brilliance; but more importantly, they have built a system where every player, coach and support staff member understands their role and how it contributes to something bigger. Their culture of shared responsibility, trust and alignment ensures success generation after generation. That's the power of a clear rudder.

I've also seen the opposite. In an Olympic support team, highly skilled professionals — physios, strength coaches and analysts — were so eager to contribute that they started stepping into each other's roles as the pressure lifted. The strength coach was giving massages, the physio was assisting in training drills and the nutritionist was offering recovery advice that conflicted with the team's broader plan. Not because they lacked ability, but because they lacked clarity.

The result? Frustration, wasted effort and inefficiencies that cost the team in critical moments. When the head coach stepped in to realign the roles, the impact was immediate — everyone had clarity, the system started flowing and the team regained its edge.

Alignment isn't about controlling people. It's freeing and empowering them to perform at their best and make their own decisions. When roles are clear, people work with confidence. Better decisions are made faster when values, purpose and principles are known. And when the whole team is aligned with the team's rudder, performance flows.

Role fit-ness

We explored fit-ness earlier, but there's another dimension that applies here. It means being fit for purpose in the role you're in, in the environment you're in, at the time you're in it. It's about alignment with the team and the demands of the role. This is where some struggle.

We often assume that if someone is skilled, experienced and successful in one role, they'll automatically succeed in another. But success doesn't transfer unless the *fit* is right. High skill doesn't always equal high impact. It's not enough to be good at something — you have to be good at what *this* role needs.

I worked with a national sports programme that had brought in a head of sports medicine from another country. On paper, they were the perfect hire — world-class in injury management, diagnosis and prevention.

But what the role *actually* needed wasn't just a top-tier clinician. It needed a leader who could bring the whole medical team together and integrate them into the wider high-performance system. Instead of stepping into that leadership role, they defaulted to what they were good at — hands-on, managing injuries and working one-on-one with athletes. The result?

Friction, confusion and a misalignment between what they were doing and what the role required.

Growing into fit-ness

The same thing happens in business. A high-performing VP was recruited from another company and brought in with the expectation that she'd grow into the new CEO. She was brilliant — highly skilled in project management, a natural organiser and great at getting things done. But her new role wasn't about managing projects; it was about leading strategy. Without realising it, she defaulted to what she knew best — supporting her team and problem-solving at a granular level — because that's what had made her successful. Her team loved her, but the business wasn't moving strategically. The fit wasn't there and she was almost released.

It wasn't for lack of skill, just a lack of awareness that what had worked in her last role wasn't what was needed in this one. When this was recognised, she adjusted. She tuned into what her new role actually required, re-aligned her focus and eventually *became* the CEO. The fitness of her role shifted from 'What I'm good at' to 'What this role needs from me right now'.

I see this happen often in sport. People move from winning systems into new teams, bringing with them what made them successful in their last role. But if they're not aware of the need to *fit* the new context, they can become disruptive, not by intention but by misalignment. They assume that what worked before will work again, without realising that the game has changed, the culture is different, and their role now requires something other than what they are delivering.

The key question is this: Are you bringing what is *fit for purpose* in this role, in this environment, at this time? Or are you bringing a *legacy* approach — clutching onto past successes that no longer fit?

Fitness in role alignment is about adaptation. The best high performers don't just apply their skills — they read the room, they understand the system and they adjust to what is actually needed. They don't cling to what made them successful *before* — they evolve to be successful *now*. Are you fit for the role you're in *today*? Or are you still playing the last game you won?

Aligning in preparation for pressure

Pressure often tests alignment in unexpected ways. When stress levels rise, teams can slip into self-preservation mode, with individuals focusing on their own responsibilities instead of the group's objectives. This misalignment can lead to inefficiencies and conflict. But when teams remain aligned, stress becomes a driver for progress.

Leaders play a crucial role in this process. They foster collaboration even under pressure by creating an environment where people feel safe to share concerns and ideas. For example, one coach I observed managed high-stakes transitions by holding regular team check-ins, ensuring everyone had a voice. These discussions addressed immediate concerns and reinforced alignment, helping the team adapt to challenges without losing focus.

Teams that thrive during transitions share a common trait of clarity. When everyone understands the purpose, their role and the broader goals, alignment becomes the foundation that sustains performance. Leaders who prioritise alignment during times of change create teams that are resilient and capable of turning challenges into opportunities for success.

Find the sweet spot

There's a point in high performance where everything clicks. A sweet spot where what people *say* and what people *do* are completely aligned. It's not just words on a page or values in a mission statement — it's in the behaviours, the habits and the culture that runs through a team like muscle memory.

The clarity vs. accountability trap

After reviewing medal-winning and non-medal-winning systems across 11 Olympic cycles, the pattern is crystal clear. The best don't just talk about alignment — they *live* it. Language and behaviour reinforce each other, and this alignment creates a performance system where people instinctively know the standards, expectations and direction without needing to second-guess.

But when that sweet spot isn't there, even the most talented teams struggle. Many leaders assume that a lack of alignment is a lack of *accountability*, so they double down on interventions, with more tracking, more reporting and more performance reviews to uncover and 'fix' the problem.

I've seen this happen in sport where leadership introduced stricter systems to improve accountability. They assumed the issue was people not taking ownership of their roles, but when we explored further, it wasn't an accountability problem at all. It was a *clarity* problem.

It's like driving at night. If the road ahead is unclear, you slow down, hesitate and second-guess your decisions. Turn on the headlights and the path is suddenly obvious. That's what happened in these teams. The moment clarity was addressed, through refining roles, reinforcing shared values and aligning what was said with what was done, accountability naturally lifted. People didn't need to be *forced* into ownership; they took it because they *could see where they were going*.

Realigning words and actions

I worked with a national team that had all the right words in place. They talked about trust, unity and playing for each other. But when things got tough, behaviours didn't match the words. Athletes trained in silos, staff operated in their own lanes and when pressure hit, fingers were pointed instead of shoulders being leaned on. Leadership initially thought it was a lack of accountability and considered putting in stricter performance measures. But once we addressed the real issue by clarifying roles, reinforcing values through daily habits and creating a culture where actions backed up words, things shifted. The sweet spot wasn't just something they aimed for; it became the way they operated.

The same applies in business. A global company I worked with had a senior leadership team that spoke about innovation and agility. They encouraged teams to take risks, experiment and push boundaries. But in practice, employees hesitated. They knew that when mistakes happened, the culture didn't *actually* reward learning — it penalised failure. The words and the reality weren't in sync, and people picked up on it fast. Again, the initial assumption was that people weren't being accountable enough, but the real issue was that people lacked *clarity* on what risk-taking actually meant in their organisation. Once leadership recognised the gap, they didn't just tweak their messaging — they changed their behaviours. They created safe spaces for experimentation, visibly celebrated lessons from failure and gave people the confidence to act on the values they had always spoken about. The shift wasn't immediate, but once it happened, the impact was undeniable.

Making alignment the norm

Championship-capable systems don't leave this to chance. They constantly tune and polish their alignment, making sure language, behaviour and habits reinforce each other. The sweet spot happens when alignment, simplicity and well-being all work together. Simplicity removes distractions so teams can focus. Well-being ensures people have the energy and resilience to sustain alignment over time. And when both of these are in place, alignment stops being something to 'work on' — it just *is*.

That's the sweet spot. The place where high performance flows, where teams move with purpose and where alignment is the culture.

AMPLIFY

Ask yourself:

- *Do I clearly understand my role and how it contributes to the bigger picture?*
- *Where is misalignment causing friction in my team, and how can we fix it?*
- *Are my daily actions and decisions aligned with my core values and my team's shared goals?*

CHAPTER 24

THE SUSTAINED PERFORMANCE GAME

To succeed, it's not enough to adjust occasionally. True sustained performance comes from building systems that embrace adaptability and anti-fragility. That means creating structures that handle uncertainty, ambiguity, challenges, transitions and setbacks and grow stronger.

The best in the game don't wait for stability — they prepare for uncertainty. They adapt, learn and evolve with their environments. These organisations succeed because they face reality as it is, not as they wish it to be. For championship-level teams, the same holds true. The most effective systems are built for transformation. That means having systems that can change and improve under pressure while staying aligned with their purpose and values. Simplicity, alignment and well-being are the anchors that keep these systems strong and flexible.

The power of anti-fragility

High performance isn't about avoiding stress, it's about using it. Anti-fragility, a concept developed by Nassim Nicholas Taleb, goes beyond resilience. Resilient systems *recover* from setbacks, but they don't necessarily improve. Robust systems are built to *withstand* pressure, but they don't change. Anti-fragile systems do something different. They *get better* under stress.

Every athlete understands this instinctively. Bones get stronger through stress. When subjected to the right amount of load — whether through impact, weight-bearing exercises or resistance training — bones don't just repair themselves; they *adapt* and become denser. Without stress, they weaken. The same is true for muscles, for skill development and for any system designed to perform at the highest level. The best don't fear stress, they condition themselves to grow from it.

The same principle applies beyond sport. The most meaningful careers, relationships and life pursuits come with challenges. Pursuing something significant always brings stress. The difference between those who sustain high performance and those who break under pressure is that the best don't just *cope* with stress — they get good at *getting better because of it*.

Anti-fragility in action

I've seen this play out across multiple Olympic cycles. The best teams sustain success over time and don't panic when things go wrong. They don't see disruption as a threat. It is simply data. An unexpected injury, a rule change or a logistical failure aren't setbacks; they're opportunities to sharpen, adjust and improve.

PART FOUR: SUSTAINING HIGH PERFORMANCE

One Olympic team I worked with had its entire preparation disrupted just weeks before a major competition. Through travel delays, lost equipment and last-minute scheduling changes, every plan they had meticulously crafted was thrown off course. Some teams unravel in such situations. They lose energy complaining, scrambling for solutions and trying to regain control. But this team had built an anti-fragile mindset long before this moment. Their approach? *'This is happening. What do we learn from it? What does this make possible?'*

They adapted. They focused on what they *could* control. And crucially, they used the chaos to sharpen their ability to handle uncertainty in competition. They didn't just recover — they competed better than before.

Contrast this with teams that *look* strong when things are going well but crumble under pressure. They rely on routine, predictability and controlled environments. The moment that control is lost, they spiral. They weren't built to get stronger from stress — they were only built to handle it when conditions were perfect.

Championship capable systems:

Predict and withstand — They prepare for disruption rather than hoping it won't come.

Recover and improve — They don't just bounce back to where they were, they refine, adjust and come back stronger.

Train for stress, not comfort — They don't avoid pressure, they build capacity to perform better under it.

This mindset applies far beyond sport. The best performance leaders always uncover a competitive advantage.

Diversity as a driver of innovation

Diversity isn't about ticking boxes. It's not limited to categories like gender, culture or background — it's about the depth and range of lived experience within a team. The best teams, the ones that sustain high performance year after year, don't just *have* diversity — they *use* it. They recognise that no single perspective is enough to navigate a complex, fast-moving world.

Diverse teams see problems before they happen. They anticipate challenges others miss, identify blind spots faster and find solutions that wouldn't have surfaced in a room full of people who think the same way. This is why high-performing teams make diversity a core part of their strategy — not for optics, but for survival and success.

The power of different lenses

I've seen this play out firsthand. In one organisation, leadership was struggling to connect with athletes on emerging social issues. They saw these concerns as distractions. Something outside of performance. But the athletes saw it differently. For them, these issues were deeply connected to identity, motivation and the bigger 'why' behind their performance. The disconnect created tension and a lack of trust.

It wasn't until leadership brought in people with broader lived experience — mentors and advisors who understood both performance *and* identity — that things started to shift. These new perspectives helped leadership see the issue through the athletes' eyes. The conversation changed. Instead of resisting, they integrated these concerns into the team's culture, strengthening alignment, purpose and, ultimately, performance. The team didn't just *cope* with change — they *adapted* faster and more effectively than their competition.

Diversity in decision-making is a competitive advantage

Diversity inside an organisation is especially critical in two areas: strategy and implementation. Without diverse perspectives at the table, strategic thinking becomes narrow, and execution lacks adaptability. The highest-performing teams make sure their leadership groups, support staff and mentors come from a range of backgrounds — not only to reflect the athletes they work with but to challenge assumptions, uncover blind spots and sharpen decision-making.

Yesterday's solutions rarely work for today's problems. Teams that succeed over time are most often learning faster than the competition. And diversity speeds up learning. A team with a range of perspectives can adapt quicker, challenge outdated thinking and evolve in ways a homogenous team never could.

This is why sustained high performance is never a solo act. Every elite athlete has a team of mentors, coaches and support staff, but the best don't surround themselves with people who think exactly like them. They bring in people who will challenge them, see the game from a different angle and force them to expand their thinking. The same applies in business, in leadership and in any high-performance system.

If you want to sustain success, you have to build diversity into the DNA of your organisation. Not as a side initiative, but as a fundamental part of how you think, plan and operate. Because in a world that's always changing, a single perspective will never be enough.

Building systems for the long game

Performance leaders create systems that make success repeatable, adaptable and built to thrive under pressure. The best systems:

Embrace reality — Adapt to the world as it is, not as you wish it to be.

Align priorities — Strip away distractions and focus on what truly drives success.

Leverage diversity — Use different perspectives to solve problems faster and spot blind spots before they appear.

Cultivate anti-fragility — Turn setbacks into fuel for growth.

Simplicity clears the noise. Alignment drives collective focus. Well-being fuels resilience. When these elements work together, high-performance systems don't just survive uncertainty, they thrive in it.

Change comes fast or slow, but it always comes. The best leaders don't wait for clarity — they create it.

PART FOUR: SUSTAINING HIGH PERFORMANCE

So ask yourself:

- *Does your system sharpen adaptability and reflect your values?*
- *Is it preparing your team to thrive in uncertainty?*

Championship-capable leaders play for the long game. The systems they create don't just achieve success — they sustain it. And that builds legacy.

PART FOUR SUMMARY

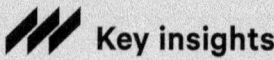 **Key insights**

High performance is environmental — Success isn't just about talent; it's about creating conditions where performance thrives. Simplicity, alignment and well-being are the pillars that sustain excellence.

Simplicity fuels clarity — The best systems remove unnecessary complexity, making it easier for individuals and teams to focus on what matters most. Less friction, more flow.

Alignment creates cohesion — Without alignment, even the most skilled teams work against themselves. Shared values, clear roles and collective direction drive sustained success.

Well-being powers performance — High performance without well-being is unsustainable. The best teams manage energy, not just time, ensuring they stay resilient and adaptable under pressure.

Anti-fragility is key — The strongest teams don't just recover from stress; they grow from it. They embrace uncertainty, adapt faster and use setbacks as fuel for progress.

Simplicity + alignment + well-being = longevity — These three elements are not separate; they reinforce each other. When all three are in place, success isn't a one-off — it's repeatable and scalable.

/// Common Blind Spots

Confusing complexity with sophistication — More layers, tools and processes don't always mean better results. The best teams simplify to amplify.

Neglecting energy management — Teams burn out when they prioritise output over recovery. Sustainable high performance comes from managing collective energy, not just workload.

Alignment assumptions — Just because an organisation has a mission statement doesn't mean people are aligned. The best revisit and reinforce values consistently.

Over-reliance on talent — Talent alone isn't enough. Without strong systems, even the best individuals struggle to sustain success over time.

Avoiding pressure and stress — Stress isn't the enemy; mismanaged stress is. The best teams embrace stress as a performance tool, not a threat.

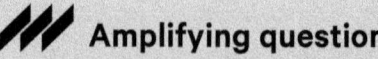 **Amplifying questions**

1. How well does my team sustain its energy, and where is it being drained?
2. Are we operating in alignment, or is friction slowing us down?
3. What unnecessary complexity can we remove to make performance flow more naturally?

PART FIVE

TOOLS AND TRAPS

High performance isn't just about having the right strategies; it's about avoiding the silent traps that can derail progress and delivery when it matters most.

Through thousands of surveys, debriefs and interviews, patterns emerged — warning signs that were visible long before a major event but often ignored. These traps don't announce themselves with a crash; they creep in subtly, draining focus, misaligning teams and sapping energy.

We've already discussed some of these traps, but Part Five is your early warning system, helping you spot and fix performance gaps before they become breaking points. We'll focus on three major performance traps:

- **Alignment traps** — When roles, goals and actions are misaligned, even the best teams struggle to sustain momentum.
- **Clarity traps** — Overcomplication, conflicting priorities and lack of focus cloud decision-making and slow execution.
- **Energy traps** — Burnout, disengagement and fatigue silently erode resilience, leading to inconsistent performance.

By understanding these traps, you'll not only avoid costly performance setbacks but also create systems that foster sustained success — built on clarity, alignment and the right energy to perform at your best when it matters most.

CHAPTER 25

ALIGNMENT TRAPS

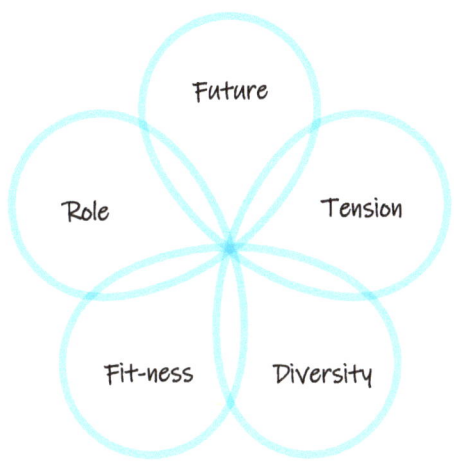

Common alignment traps

Alignment is the glue that holds high-performing teams together. Without it, even the best individuals struggle to function as a unit. The following five common traps were repeatedly cited as the cause of performance breakdowns — often seen too late. Here's what they are and how to fix them.

A foggy vision creates a lost team

A team without a shared vision is like a ship without a compass — drifting, reactive and misaligned. Without a clear, well-articulated direction, people interpret success differently and pull in competing directions. The best leaders ensure vision isn't just understood — it's owned and lived by every team member.

→ **Fix it:** Regularly revisit and reinforce the vision. Make it part of daily language, not just a document in a drawer.

Conflict tension vs. constructive tension

> **Conflict is personal. Constructive tension is purposeful.**

Some teams become consumed by unproductive conflict, draining energy, creating division and shifting focus from performance to politics. But the best teams embrace constructive tension, using differing perspectives to drive innovation, sharpen decision-making and fuel progress. The key difference? Conflict is personal. Constructive tension is purposeful.

→ **Fix it:** Reframe friction as a driver of progress. Set ground rules for healthy debate and ensure challenges are about the work — not the person.

Relying on categories instead of lived experience

Diversity isn't about ticking boxes, it's about valuing lived experience. Too often, teams see diversity as an exercise in representation rather than integration. High performers go beyond labels, recognising that different experiences bring unique insights that strengthen collective intelligence.

→ **Fix it:** Create space for real conversations. Don't assume inclusion. Actively seek out and integrate different perspectives into decision-making.

Blurred roles cause bottlenecks

When team members aren't crystal clear on their role (or the roles of others), frustration and inefficiency take hold. Misalignment leads to duplication of effort, gaps in execution and confusion over accountability. The best teams don't just define roles — they constantly refine them as needs evolve.

→ **Fix it:** Clarify who owns what. Regularly review roles to ensure responsibilities match reality and eliminate overlap.

Team fit-ness vs. individual brilliance

A collection of talent isn't the same as a high-performing team. Many teams fail because they prioritise star performers over fit — leading to imbalance, friction and inconsistency. True fit-ness isn't about sameness; it's about finding complementary strengths that create a cohesive unit.

→ **Fix it:** Don't just recruit for skill — recruit for synergy. A high-performing team is more than the sum of its parts.

How these traps interconnect

I worked with an Olympic support team before the Paris Games. On paper, they had world-class expertise, yet they were struggling. Initially, it seemed like a role clarity issue as multiple staff members were stepping on each other's toes. But digging deeper, we found the real issue was a missing shared vision.

Without a clear North Star, team members were defining success in their own ways, leading to role confusion, unproductive conflict and misaligned priorities. This lack of clarity blocked collaboration and weakened trust.

Once we addressed the root cause by creating a shared vision and aligning roles, the entire system shifted. Tension became constructive, contributions became more valuable and the team operated as a unit, not just a collection of individuals.

Just like the Olympic rings, these traps are interconnected. Fixing one without addressing the others, only creates temporary solutions. High-performance leadership means tackling them as a system — ensuring clarity, alignment and fit at every level.

Ask yourself:

- *Are we truly working toward the same goal, or just assuming we are?*
- *Do I turn challenges into growth opportunities or let tension divide us?*
- *Are we a high-performing team moving as one, or just talented individuals working in parallel?*

Recognise these early. Fix them fast. That's how alignment fuels sustained high performance.

CHAPTER 26

CLARITY TRAPS

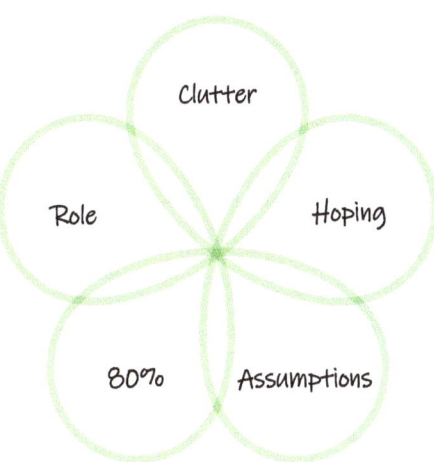

Clarity is the foundation of high performance, yet it's often the first thing to get lost under pressure. Instead of sharp focus, teams get caught in the clutter of busyness, outdated assumptions and a false sense of progress. These clarity traps don't appear overnight — they accumulate quietly, shaping cultures, decisions and habits until they silently sabotage performance.

Common clarity traps

The best teams and leaders are relentless in protecting clarity. Here are five common clarity traps that can derail performance and what to do about them.

Busyness masquerading as progress

Being busy feels productive, but it's not the same as making progress. Clogged calendars, endless meetings and reactive task-switching create an illusion of momentum while draining focus from the real work that drives results.

> **➜ Fix it:** Cut the clutter. Challenge every meeting, report and task. If it doesn't drive impact, then eliminate, delegate or streamline it. Create space for deep work instead of mistaking movement for progress.

Hoping vs. knowing

Hope is not a strategy. Too many teams operate on hope. Hoping things will improve, hoping their plans will work, hoping that alignment will happen organically. The best teams remove guesswork. They test, measure, refine and operate with certainty, not wishful thinking.

> **➜ Fix it:** Turn hope into a plan. Ask: *What do we know for sure? What do we need to test?* Make decisions based on evidence, not assumptions.

Assumptions that create blind spots

Every team has unquestioned assumptions. These are long-standing habits or beliefs that no one challenges. The problem? What worked before may no longer serve you now. Assumptions create invisible constraints that limit adaptability and innovation.

> **➜ Fix it:** Regularly audit your assumptions. Ask, '*What are we taking for granted that might be holding us back?*'

Bring in outside perspectives to uncover blind spots you can't see from the inside.

Focusing on the 80%

The Pareto Principle teaches that 80% of results come from just 20% of effort — yet too many teams stay buried in low-impact work. The truly elite take it further, honing in on the vital 10% — the small, decisive actions that drive disproportionate success.

→ **Fix it:** Identify the high-impact 10% — the decisions, habits and efforts that truly shape success. Eliminate, automate or delegate everything else. Protect the 10% that matters most.

Unclear standards of behaviour

Goals alone don't drive performance — standards of behaviour do. Teams without clear, shared standards drift into inconsistency. Confusion rises. Performance fluctuates. The best teams operate with non-negotiable standards that create alignment, trust and consistency under pressure.

→ **Fix it:** Define and reinforce daily behaviours that support performance. Ask: *What behaviours must be present every day for us to win?* Make them visible, explicit and accountable.

How the traps interconnect

Just like the Olympic rings, these clarity traps don't exist in isolation — they overlap. Unclear standards lead to busyness.

Assumptions lead to misplaced focus. A lack of strategy turns knowing into hoping.

The best leaders tune into these connections and fix them before they break performance. Addressing one strengthens the whole system, creating a ripple effect of focus, alignment and sustained success.

Ask yourself:

- *Am I busy, or am I actually making progress on what matters most?*
- *Am I relying on hope and assumptions, or do I have clear, tested actions in place?*
- *Am I focusing my energy on the vital 10% or getting lost in the 80% that doesn't move the needle?*

Clarity is a performance multiplier. Protect it. Sharpen it. It will drive your success.

CHAPTER 27

ENERGY TRAPS

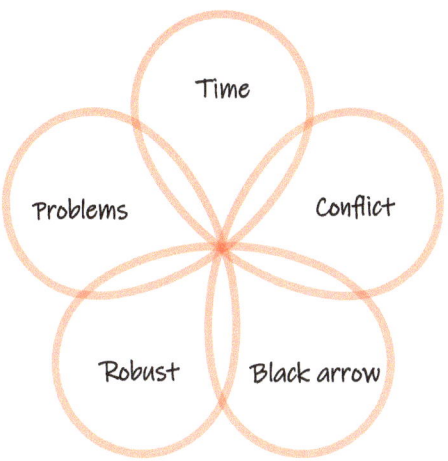

Energy is the fuel that drives high performance, but many teams unknowingly drain their reserves by falling into energy traps. These traps aren't always obvious at first. They build gradually, sapping focus, momentum and resilience until teams find themselves exhausted and reactive rather than proactive and adaptive. Recognising and avoiding these hidden drains is a critical skill for leaders who want to sustain performance over time.

AMPLIFY

Common energy traps

Running out of time

Time optimism is one of the most common energy traps. It is the belief that there is always more time than there actually is. Teams overcommit, overestimate what they can achieve and then scramble at the last minute. The real issue isn't time management — it's energy management. Time is finite, but energy can be replenished. High performers pace themselves, protect recovery time and avoid the burnout cycle of pushing hard, collapsing and repeating the pattern.

→ **Fix it:** Set and protect realistic timeframes. Shift from managing time to managing energy. Ask: *Are we sprinting towards exhaustion or pacing for sustained performance?*

Conflict resolution over root cause empowerment

Many teams mistake resolving conflicts for progress. Instead of addressing the real issues, they smooth things over, only for the same tensions to resurface later. This constant firefighting drains energy and trust. Instead of merely fixing disputes, strong leaders empower teams to tackle the deeper, systemic issues at play. The best teams don't just resolve conflict — they evolve because of it.

→ **Fix it:** Go beyond surface-level solutions — find the root cause of recurring tensions. Ask: *Are we solving the real issue, or just managing symptoms?*

Reacting to the wrong problems

It's easy to get distracted by problems that feel urgent but aren't truly significant. This is the Black Arrow effect, where leaders chase minor issues, diverting attention from what really matters. This constant reactivity keeps teams in a state of firefighting rather than focused progress. High performers stay locked on the bigger picture, channelling energy where it will have the most impact rather than where the next distraction appears.

→ **Fix it:** Pause before reacting. Define what truly drives success. Ask: *Is this a critical priority, or just noise?*

Perpetual problem-solving vs. creating and empowering

Teams that spend all their time solving problems become trapped in a reactive loop. If the focus is always on fixing, then creativity, ownership and innovation take a backseat. The best teams shift from being fixers to being creators. Instead of solving the same issues repeatedly, they design environments where problems are prevented, and people feel empowered to take action without waiting for permission.

→ **Fix it:** Shift from problem-solving to proactive creation. Ask: *Are we building a system where people can take action without waiting for leadership?*

Rigid systems vs. antifragile systems

A rigid system might look strong, but it breaks under pressure. The best teams aren't just resilient; they're antifragile. They don't just withstand stress — they grow stronger from it. Instead of locking into rigid rules and overly structured processes, high performers build adaptive systems that flex, evolve and thrive in uncertainty.

These energy traps don't exist in isolation. Poor time management leads to rushed conflict resolution, which fuels the Black Arrow of distraction. That, in turn, keeps teams locked in problem-solving mode rather than proactive innovation, reinforcing rigidity instead of adaptability. Addressing just one of these traps can free up energy, creating a ripple effect that strengthens the entire system.

→ **Fix it:** Build adaptability into processes and mindsets. Ask: *Are we designed to grow through disruption, or are we stuck in outdated ways of working?*

How the traps interconnect

Energy traps don't exist in isolation. They compound, feeding off each other in a cycle that drains performance. Running out of time leads to rushed decisions and firefighting. Conflict avoidance creates unresolved tension, further depleting energy reserves. Reacting to the wrong problems shifts focus away from what truly matters, increasing frustration and fatigue. Teams trapped in perpetual problem-solving become stuck in survival mode, leaving little space for proactive thinking or innovation.

Performance leaders recognise these interconnections early. Fixing just one trap — whether it's protecting recovery time, addressing root causes instead of symptoms or shifting from reactive to proactive — can free up energy and create a ripple effect. When teams move from exhaustion to strategic energy management, they don't just sustain performance — they amplify it.

Ask yourself:

- *Am I managing my energy wisely, or am I always running on empty?*
- *Do I keep fixing the same problems, or am I empowering my team to prevent them?*
- *Is my team built to adapt and thrive under pressure, or are we stuck in rigid, outdated ways of working?*

Energy is the currency of high performance. Protect it, to empower your people and system to flow.

CHAPTER 28

A CALL TO PERFORMANCE LEADERSHIP

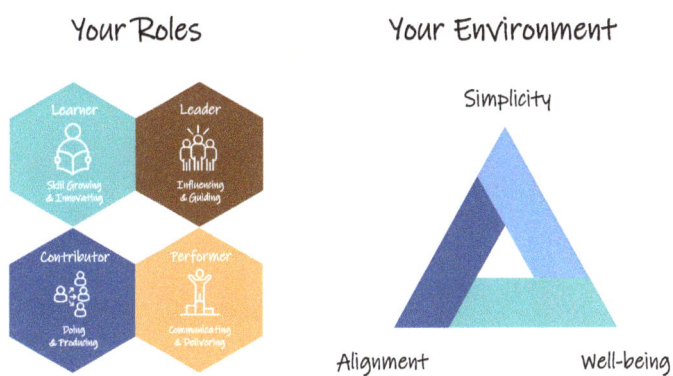

Revisiting the challenge

From the first page of this book, we've explored the foundations of high performance — not just in sport but in leadership, teams and systems. We've tackled the common traps that hold us back in the systems we create and the roles we play. At its heart, this journey has been about one fundamental question.

What does it take to create sustained high performance, consistently, over time?

The hard truth for many is that most people don't struggle because they lack ambition, effort or talent. They stagnate or oscillate because their systems are working against them, not for them.

> **High performance is proportional to impact, not effort.**

High performance is about people and communication. We've seen that high performance is proportional to impact, not effort. The best moved from working hard to working better. It's about alignment, clarity, simplicity and well-being. It's about moving beyond raw talent and quick wins to designing systems and habits that create repeatable excellence.

The master model

Throughout this book, we've returned to the three pillars of sustained high performance:

Simplicity cuts through complexity and focuses only on what truly matters.

Alignment ensures that every role, habit and system pulls in the same direction.

Well-being creates a foundation of energy, resilience and adaptability that sustains performance over the long term.

When simplicity, alignment and well-being are in place, we amplify our leadership, our teams and our results. We remove friction, avoid burnout and drive lasting success.

But theory isn't enough. High performance lives in action. It's in the choices we make, the conversations we have and the way we shape our teams and environments.

Your role in the system

Through this journey, we've identified four core roles that sustain high performance:

Leaders set the direction and shape the culture.

Learners embrace adaptability and continuous improvement.

Contributors create momentum through action and collaboration.

Performers execute under pressure, delivering results when it matters most.

No matter where you are in your journey, you play all four roles at different times. The key is to know which role to step into at any given moment, and to design systems that enable everyone around you to do the same.

This is the essence of performance leadership: knowing when to lead, when to learn, when to contribute and when to execute. All while creating an environment where others can thrive, too.

My challenge to you

The book may be ending, but your leadership journey is not. So, I'll leave you with three questions to guide your next steps:

- *What's the one habit, system or mindset shift you can implement today that would have the biggest impact on your performance?*
- *How can you better align your role, your team and your environment to create sustained high performance?*
- *Who can you empower to move from problem-solving to possibility-creating?*

High performance isn't just about what you do. It's about the systems you build, the roles you play and the impact you leave behind.

How you can engage further

If this book has resonated with you, don't let the conversation end here. Start a movement in your team or workplace.

Apply the framework

Start small. Focus on one principle, whether it's simplifying your approach, creating better alignment or prioritising well-being, and see what changes.

Connect with others

High performance isn't built in isolation. Who in your team or network is on this journey with you?

PART FIVE: TOOLS AND TRAPS

Stay curious

Keep learning, refining and adapting. Sustained excellence comes from a mindset of continuous improvement.

You can find more insights, tools and resources at https://simplify2perform and https://richardnyoung.com, where we continue to unlock how to amplify leadership and performance.

Final thoughts

At the start of this book, I said that leadership is a choice, not a title. It's the moment-to-moment decisions we make about where to focus, how to lead and how to align ourselves with what truly matters.

And now, that choice is in your hands.

Step onto the bridge with clarity. Shape your system with intent. Empower yourself and those around you. The work of high performance isn't about waiting — it's about stepping forward, every day, with purpose.

So, what will you amplify next?

SUPPORT FROM HERE

You'll find plenty of resources to empower your high performance leadership journey at https://Simplify2Perform.com and https://richardnyoung.com

Free Resources

1. **Insight Papers**

   Explore summary insights from real-world medallists and non-medallists.

2. **Performance Diagnostics**

   Access practical tools to explore and measure key elements of your performance leadership.

3. **Weekly Insights & Newsletter Archive**

   Get real-world stories, tools and reflections delivered straight to your inbox every week — or browse the full newsletter library.

SUPPORT FROM HERE

Ongoing Programmes to Amplify your Leadership

Take what you've learned in *Amplify* and bring it to life through targeted, high-impact experiences that create lasting transformation.

- **The Amplify Leadership Profile**

  Your personal performance map.

- **1:1 or Group Mentoring**

  Clarity meets accountability.

- **Performance Workshops (Half-Day or Full-Day)**

  Hands-on sessions to dive deeper into the principles of *Amplify*, with immediate application to your leadership, team dynamics and system design.

- **The Masterclass Series**

  Learn, connect, grow — together.

  Join a cohort or bring your own team to explore focused themes over eight weeks. Each masterclass is practical, high-trust and built for real-world change.

- **Amplify Keynote Menu**

  Spark the shift.

  Choose from a range of thought-provoking keynotes designed to inspire, challenge and activate the performance mindset in any setting — from boardrooms to conferences.

MEET RICHARD YOUNG

Richard Young has spent four decades at the forefront of high-performance sport, working across 11 Olympic cycles, including many World Cups, World Championships and International Games, shaping the success of athletes, teams, leaders and organisations in over 50 sports and businesses across seven countries. A former Olympic team member for Canada and Pan American Games gold medallist and coach of world champions, Richard has played a pivotal role in designing and leading world-class performance systems.

His impact spans multiple national Olympic teams, including two Olympic cycles with Team GB, three with New Zealand and international collaborations across seven other nations. He has initiated six groundbreaking programmes for international sport preparation in three countries, integrating expertise from elite sport, military strategy, Formula 1 and leading research to drive sustained high performance.

MEET RICHARD YOUNG

Richard is renowned for capturing and distilling the lived experiences of elite athletes, coaches and performance leaders. He has documented the behaviours, decisions and environments that enable repeat medallists, shaping evidence-based approaches that accelerate learning and maximise potential in individuals and teams. His work has directly contributed to multiple Olympic and World Championship medals, influencing the way high-performance environments are designed and sustained.

Originally trained in physiology, Richard went on to study an M.Sc. in biomedical engineering at McGill University and earned a PhD in medical science from the University of Calgary. His deep expertise in human performance and his ability to translate complexity into simple, actionable frameworks have made him a trusted advisor to elite athletes, sports organisations and business leaders seeking to perform under pressure.

Richard's journey is also deeply personal. He met his wife, Donna, at an IOC sports conference in Olympia, Greece. After her premature passing in 2021, he has continued his work with a commitment to developing performance systems that support not only success but also well-being. Based in Dunedin, New Zealand, he is the father of four children and remains dedicated to helping individuals and teams unlock their highest potential.

FURTHER READING

Brown, B. (2018). *Dare to Lead: Brave work. Tough conversations. Whole hearts.* Random House.
- Explores vulnerability, trust and courageous leadership.

Burkeman, O. (2021). *Four Thousand Weeks: Time management for mortals.* Farrar, Straus and Giroux.
- Challenges traditional productivity thinking and encourages meaningful focus.

Clear, J. (2018). *Atomic Habits: An easy & proven way to build good habits & break bad ones.* Avery.
- A practical guide to habit formation and sustainable performance improvement.

Collins, J. (2001). *Good to Great: Why some companies make the leap...and others don't.* HarperBusiness.
- Examines what distinguishes high-performing organisations from the rest.

Eastwood, O. (2021). *Belonging: The ancient code of togetherness.* Quercus.
- Highlights the power of connection, culture and identity in performance.

Hardy, B., & Sullivan, D. (2023). *10x is easier than 2x: How world-class entrepreneurs achieve more by doing less.* Hay House.
- Focuses on strategic simplicity and making bigger leaps with less effort.

FURTHER READING

Kahneman, D. (2011). *Thinking, Fast and Slow*. Farrar, Straus and Giroux.
- Explains how decision-making biases impact performance and leadership.

Kerr, J. (2013). *Legacy: What the All Blacks can teach us about the business of life*. Constable.
- Lessons from one of the most successful sports teams on leadership and culture.

McKeown, G. (2014). *Essentialism: The disciplined pursuit of less*. Crown Business.
- Advocates for focusing on what truly matters by eliminating distractions.

Pink, D. H. (2009). *Drive: The surprising truth about what motivates us*. Riverhead Books.
- Explores motivation, autonomy and mastery as drivers of high performance.

Taleb, N. N. (2012). *Antifragile: Things that gain from disorder*. Random House.
- A deep dive into resilience and thriving under uncertainty.

Willink, J., & Babin, L. (2015). *Extreme Ownership: How U.S. Navy SEALs lead and win*. St. Martin's Press.
- A leadership framework based on accountability under pressure.

REFERENCES

1. Clear, J. (2018). *Atomic Habits: An easy & proven way to build good habits & break bad ones.* Avery.
2. Sinek, S. (2009). *Start With Why: How great leaders inspire everyone to take action.* London: Penguin.
3. Dweck, C. (2012). *Mindset: How You Can Fulfil Your Potential.* London: Constable & Robinson.
4. Kerr, J. (2013). *Legacy: What the All Blacks can Teach Us About the Business of Life.* London: Constable.
5. Kahneman, D. (2011). *Thinking, fast and slow.* Farrar, Straus and Giroux.
6. Evans, C. (2020). *Perform Under Pressure.* HarperCollins NZ ed.
7. Peters, S. (2012). *The Chimp Paradox: the mind management program to help you achieve success, confidence, and happiness.* New York: Jeremy P. Tarcher/Penguin.
8. De Geus, A. (2002). *The Living Company.* Boston, Mass.: Harvard Business School Press.
9. Kahneman, D. (2011). *Thinking, Fast and Slow.* Farrar, Straus and Giroux.
10. De Geus, A. (2002). *The Living Company.* Boston, Mass.: Harvard Business School Press.
11. Benner, P. (1984). *From Novice to Expert: Excellence and power in clinical nursing practice.* Addison-Wesley.

REFERENCES

12. Brown, B. (2018). *Dare to lead: Brave work, tough conversations, whole hearts.* New York: Random House.

13. Sullivan, D. & Hardy, B. (2023). *10x Is Easier Than 2x.* Hay House, Inc.

14. aon.com. (n.d.). *2022-2023 Global Wellbeing Survey | Aon.* [online] Available at: https://www.aon.com/global-wellbeing-survey.

15. Jeffery, B., Weddle, B., Brassey, J. and Thaker, S. (2025). *Thriving workplaces: How employers can improve productivity and change lives.* [online] McKinsey & Company. Available at: https://www.mckinsey.com/mhi/our-insights/thriving-workplaces-how-employers-can-improve-productivity-and-change-lives.

16. Inc, G. (2023). *Help Your Employees Cope With Stress.* [online] Gallup.com. Available at: https://www.gallup.com/workplace/509726/help-employees-cope-stress.aspx.

17. Csikszentmihalyi, M. (1990). *Flow: The psychology of optimal experience.* Harper & Row.

www.ingramcontent.com/pod-product-compliance
Lightning Source LLC
Chambersburg PA
CBHW040245010526
44119CB00057B/821